FROM EVEREST TO
THE SOUTH POLE

FROM EVEREST TO

THE SOUTH POLE

By GEORGE LOWE

ILLUSTRATED

ST MARTIN'S PRESS · NEW YORK

CONTENTS

ILLUSTRATIONS

Hannes la Grange
Hal Lister
Roy Homard and David Pratt fishing through a hole in the
ice during a winter snowstorm

Following page 136

Taffy Williams
John Lewis
Allan Rogers
Ralph Lenton
Peter Weston
Geoff Pratt
Gordon Haslop
Jon Stephenson

Following page 176

David Stratton
Bunny Fuchs
David Pratt
Sno-Cat in the first crevasse
The Polar Plateau. Jon Stephenson's team the day before
reaching the Pole, and Sno-Cats at 10,000 feet after leaving
the Pole
The Skelton Glacier. Hal Lister breaking camp in high wind,
and two Sno-Cats, a mile apart, hurrying down the Glacier
Ed Hillary and myself on arrival at Scott Base

MAPS AND PLANS

CHAPTER I

The Map on the Wall

FORTY years after the death of Scott and his companions, a small proud club of men were meeting annually in London—always on a Friday of January, somewhere near the anniversary of Scott's arrival at the South Pole in 1912. This was the celebration dinner of the exclusive Antarctic Club, and in 1954 I found myself among the one hundred and fifty guests and members.

The occasion happened to coincide with my thirtieth birthday, but that was not the factor making me conscious of a certain strangeness in the atmosphere; nor was it caused by the stimulus of my first attendance in the distinguished company. The fact was I was reflecting that although forty years does not represent much in the history of exploration I had nevertheless grown up to think of Captain Scott in the same timeless vacuum as Marco Polo, Columbus or Livingstone. The Antarctic continent meant little or nothing to my mind, and like any sixth-former of the present day I saw Antarctica only in its historical context along with the ghostly figures of Scott, Wilson, Evans, Oates and Bowers stumbling through a whirling snowstorm.

It now came as a sharp surprise to be suddenly face to face with men who had actually been south with Scott.

While the port was passed I watched the glistening faces, saw

1

the old and young moving in their chairs to an accompaniment of tinkling glasses and the occasional jangle of rows of medals. Then the heavy decanter reached me, and as I lifted it my distinguished neighbour said: 'Have you ever tried to share a tent with a raving lunatic? I remember one dreadful night back in . . .'

He got no further. A pink-coated toastmaster, ready for his brief hour of dictatorship, brought all anecdotes to a full stop. 'Gentlemen!' he boomed. 'The President desires to take wine with the members of the 1901–1903 *Discovery* Expedition.'

Whereupon the noise of a chair scraping in a far corner made the whole assembly turn. The President, beaming from the top table, stood with glass poised, pointing it towards the distant corner. The chair scraped again, and the knives and forks clattered as a very old man struggled with difficulty to his feet.

His back was bent and his medals rattled and his glass shook as he raised it. A burst of applause broke out. The old surviving member drank, then settled back heavily into his chair. The rest of us sipped in tribute.

'Who is he?' I whispered to my neighbour.

'That's Admiral Skelton,' he hissed. 'He was with Scott's first.'

The toastmaster intoned once more. 'Gentlemen, the President desires to take wine with the members of the 1908–1909 Shackleton Expedition.'

Leaping up, the President toasted three more bemedalled ageing members who rose very slowly. Their honourable and honoured figures were no less vigorously applauded.

And yet another . . . 'Gentlemen, the President desires to take wine with the members of . . .'

I was fascinated as the ceremony continued through every Antarctic expedition during the fifty-four years of the century, the President performing his duties ten or twelve times with, so to speak, an explorer's doggedness. It was a living parade of history, and I thought all these people were dead.

2

Then suddenly . . . 'Gentlemen, the President desires to take wine with the member of the successful Everest Expedition of 1953.'

Good Lord, that's me, I remembered, and blushing at the surprise I got to my feet while the President, now glowing and rubicund, surveyed me from his table. I stood with *my* glass held shoulder high, the President rose for the toast, drank gallantly, and crashed into his seat to another roar of applause.

Wishing for the comforting presence of my Everest colleagues, I finished my port in silence, knowing that my old friend Ed Hillary, now the harassed Sir Edmund, was giving a lecture somewhere else in England; for one reason or another I was the sole 'surviving' Everest climber for the Antarctic Club guest list.

A few weeks before the dinner I had met Dr. Vivian Fuchs for the first time, introduced by Fuchs's own guide and mentor Sir James Wordie at the Royal Geographical Society. Our paths crossed once or twice again during 1954, and even the magic words Trans-Antarctic Expedition were breathed. But still the notion of myself in the role of Antarctic explorer was remote, to say the least. Above all else I was a climber, a mountaineer. Some men enjoy going 'up'; others choose the hard frozen Antarctic flatness and the conquering of its horizontal hazards. I belonged to the school that generally prefers going 'up'.

It was not till November of the same year that Bunny Fuchs presented me with a confidential foolscap document which I placed carefully in my briefcase.

'That's the detailed plan,' said Bunny. 'Take it away and see what you can make of it. If you will also write to Ed Hillary and sound him out, I'd be glad. I want to know if I can get a New Zealand party interested.'

He twisted his pipe, relit it with his petrol lighter, then added: 'And if this comes off—would *you* want to go with Ed?'

There was a pause while I pondered hard and quickly, thinking that if I went on the expedition, I would prefer to be with the main party crossing the Antarctic continent. 'I should like to make the complete crossing,' I said at last, 'if you will have me.'

'I want a New Zealander,' said Bunny.

'That's me—but what else would I be?' I asked.

'I want not only a mountaineer, but one who can also look after the photography,' said Bunny.

'Photographer and New Zealand liaison officer,' I reflected. 'That'll do for me.'

'Interpreter, too,' said Bunny laconically.

'Of what?' I asked.

'New Zealand messages,' he said.

We shook hands, I hopped on a bus, went to my bed-sitting-room at Earl's Court, pinned a large map of Antarctica to the dingy Victorian wallpaper—and began studying the foolscap folder that was labelled *Plans for a Trans-Antarctic Journey, by V. E. Fuchs, M.A., Ph.D.*

Up to this moment I had never been absolutely certain about my desire or willingness to commit myself for an expedition that would spread over the lengthy span of three years. Projects for climbing even the highest mountains were usually reckoned in months, not years, and in my world the Pole venture was an altogether new idea that took some getting used to.

Perhaps I would never have reached a firm decision without the spur of a certain shadowy mental picture that somehow kept blurring the great Antarctic map on the wall. Every day it came. A kind of back projection that fixed into the map not only the figures of Scott, Shackleton, Byrd, Amundsen, but also those of the elderly gentlemen who rose to their feet that night of the Antarctic dinner. The old survivors, indeed, rather than the historic hero leaders, made the icebound continent come truly alive, or at any rate fired the new enthusiasm for the Polar regions that was gradually growing inside me.

*   *   *

4

When I was nine or ten years old I was impressed by a remarkable film called *The Great White South*. Shot, directed and most of it actually processed in the Antarctic by its remarkable creator Herbert Ponting, it told the story of Scott's dramatic 1912 expedition. Ponting, who justifiably called himself a camera artist, travelled with the Scott party on their great adventure.

It would be pleasant but untrue to draw the significant conclusion that as a schoolboy of the nineteen-thirties I sat enthralled through the film (which I did) and was henceforth captivated by the dream of an Antarctic crossing (which I was not). I was not even a climber until well past my twenty-first birthday, at which point I was still terrified by heights, a fear that was shared and possibly transferred to me by my mother. And this nervous dislike of heights, together with the results of a schooldays accident that smashed my left arm, was without a doubt the real cause of my paradoxical embrace of a pastime that was sensibly shunned by all other members of the enormous family to which I belonged.

I was not merely the seventh of eight children, I was the seventh child of a seventh child. My mother and father both hailed from families containing twelve children, and the pattern created by countless weddings currently blesses me with forty-eight uncles and aunts, one hundred and twenty first cousins and, at the last reckoning, twenty-two nieces and nephews. In and around the New Zealand farming community of Hastings, on North Island, where I was born, it was regarded as traditional and inevitable that all the Lowes, or at least the males among them, should enter one branch or another of the staple New Zealand farming industries—butter, meat and wool, or market gardening. My own father was a fruit farmer.

The family tradition was punctured on a certain sunny day of 1934.

This was a year when the knight errant of aviation was the pioneer long-distance flyer Charles Kingsford Smith. He was then barnstorming New Zealand on a fund-raising mission a year before the fatal trans-Pacific flight from which he did not return, and our parents were taking us to see him on the Sunday of his visit to Hastings.

After an early lunch I stood on the veranda, hands in my trousers pockets, idly surveying two of my brothers engaged in a friendly bout of boxing; a mixture, rather, of horseplay, fisti-cuffs and breathless chase.

Suddenly they cannoned right into me, and the day was turned into a disaster before it had even begun. I fell headlong off the veranda steps, crashed heavily on my left side, and woke up in the sitting-room with a broken arm giving considerable pain. The day's outing was cancelled. Our regular family doctor happened to be on holiday, so another man was called in and he, a young newcomer to the district, got to work on my fracture, which was just above the elbow, while my brothers stood by, full of contrition.

The afternoon passed gloomily. We were a sombre set of brothers who went to bed that night, Arch and Jock at home and I in a local nursing home where I spent the next week.

And for eighteen months afterwards I was in constant trouble. The arm would not mend. The complications involved a long series of operations, the arm being continually broken, set, re-broken and set again, usually on the dining-room table. For a year and a half I missed most of my schooling.

I would listen miserably and with rising resentment to whispered conferences with the doctor. 'It looks pretty hopeless' . . . 'He'll never use that arm' . . . 'Afraid he'll always be a bit of a cripple' . . . 'A manual job is out of the question' . . . 'Physically, not much use' . . . 'Better give him a decent educa-tion . . . maybe a career where he can use his brains' . . . and so on.

The effect of all this was that my parents took very seriously at least one part of the varied advice. They kept me at school till I was almost twenty, four or five years past the age when my brothers and cousins graduated to the farm. I went on to the teachers' training college and university—and at twenty-two, qualified, became a teacher at the Hastings primary school I had attended as a boy. Then, and to this day, my left arm developed virtually without muscle, and though its movements were restricted I found myself silently resolving that I would disprove the doctor's damnable prophecies about my being a cripple 'for life'.

This determination was somewhat hampered, I must add, by the broad streak of cowed and cowardly feeling which still gripped my entrails whenever I was called on to show even a slight degree of athletic initiative. A vivid recollection of my university days concerns a Sunday walk along some cliffs where, at one point, the path narrowed to a yard in width, with a sheer drop on either side. Heaven knows the path was safe enough, yet at twenty-one I was stricken with fear and felt utterly sickened by the failure of my effort to teeter across.

If anyone had that day told me I would be shooting a film near the very peak of Everest less than eight years ahead, and wagered a thousand pounds on it into the bargain, I would certainly have accepted the bet. All the same, the popular concept of 'fearlessness' is often misplaced. Without fear you will not, I believe, go very high on a mountain. Naturally the fear must be handled, mastered, controlled—the 'self', if you like, conquered. But the harebrained 'fearless' are always unreliable and generally unsuccessful. During our first big climb together, Ed Hillary told me: 'I don't think a climb is really worth while unless you have been scared out of your wits at least twice.' The theory is less masochistic than it sounds, and the feelings of high contentment, of elation, produced by various skills that now make it possible for me to climb, are to some extent governed by this 'controlled' fear. A good deal of conscious training and mental effort were needed to overcome the worst phases, but in terms of plain enjoyment the results were, in the end, worth all the strain and trying. Imperceptibly the

7

conscious act of control becomes a catalyst, transforming mortal terror into manageable tension—an exercise in a school of emotional *yogi* which can be satisfying provided you do not become the victim of that indefinable process known to extroverts as 'unhealthy' introspection.

As things turned out it was a young man of decidedly introspective and adventurous spirit who was responsible for my first essays in climbing. Geoffrey Milne, one of my training college fraternity, suggested one day in 1945 that we should try to organize for ourselves a working holiday in the mountain region of South Island. To set the scheme in motion we wrote to the New Zealand Tourist Association offering our services, for suitable reward, in the work of recutting a famous track through the bush country, the overgrown Milford track. To our surprise this proposal was promptly accepted, and emboldened by success we wrote again to inquire, in effect, what else they had to offer. Straightaway came a reply informing us that we could go, if we wished, to the Mount Cook area—the Zermatt of New Zealand—to work as assistants with the professional guides who were starting to re-equip and make ready the mountain huts for post-war climbers. Delighted with our luck, Geoffrey and I decided to hand over the Milford track-cutting vacation to any of our friends who were interested, while *we* chose the still more attractive Mount Cook assignment.

And off we went, for six glorious weeks, receiving £20 each for our trouble. I was twenty-two, it was my first sight of mountains, my first real trip away from home, and my first visit to South Island; it seemed that life was just beginning.

Above all, we learned from these experts who were the professional mountaineers a sound and sensible attitude towards the problems of travelling in mountain territory. Early each morning I would set off in company with a guide and sometimes a party of tourists who were being taken on to the glacier. Neither they nor I had ever before seen a glacier, but by keeping a superior silence about my ignorance I found the tourists were soon regarding me as an experienced professional, a gargantuan error which I made no attempt to correct. By the end of our six weeks' stay I had distinctly inflated feelings, an unprecedented physical fitness, and a genuine passion for the mountain country. For one as impressionable as I was the experience was like the watering of a plant; the guides seemed to like me and I soaked up their hints and information with speed and great enthusiasm.

Under the guidance of men like Mick Bowie and Harry Ayres in particular we became steeped in the thought and philosophy of mountaineering. We came to know that the ice-covered mountains were not unchanging, inanimate structures, but malleable shapes that could move with the seasons, become soft or hard, closed or open, granulated or glassy, have moods and were alive if not exactly breathing.

Twelve months later, during another school holiday, we were back again at Mount Cook. Meantime, at home on North Island, I went on my first expeditions in miniature, at weekends, and with a group of friends climbed my first mountain— the 9,176-foot volcano called Ruapehu, which in English means Two Noses.

CHAPTER II

Any Two Can Join Us

THE mountain bus was an ungainly affair, a big, brown, rubber-tyred creature with a high wheelbase, transporting us along rough tracks from the Mount Cook hotel, across the floor of a valley, through a wilderness of boulders, over dry stream beds and right up to the side of the glacier, there to disgorge its loads of climbers and tourists. It was not long before I was regularly conducting parties of sightseers on their first visits to the glacier, cutting steps, guiding them to some interesting point after alighting from the bus. But always I enjoyed the rattling bus ride, too, for the view of the valley and mountains was superb.

One day I noticed a long-limbed, keen-faced young man sitting alone on the rear seat. Dressed in old tweed trousers with puttees around the ankles, a tartan shirt with a sweat rag circling his neck, all topped by a battered brown ski cap, he carried an ice-axe and a small rucksack, and his green eyes roved with a curious excitement over the scenery. I joined him at the back of the bus, and we talked easily about the mountains. The excited, ever-interested look never left his eyes. He had been a war-time navigator on bombers, was four years my senior, and was now working for his father who kept a bee farm in Auckland.

'My father runs a fruit farm,' I told him, 'with bee-keeping as a sideline. As a matter of fact we get our queen bees from a chap in Auckland—someone called Hillary.'

'That's us,' said the young man. 'My name's Ed Hillary. Small world, isn't it?'

We joked a bit about the coincidence, but just as we were getting to know each other the bus jolted to a stop. Hillary had a rendezvous with a climbing friend at a hut somewhere up the glacier. We exchanged addresses and shook hands.

'Let's do a climb together, maybe next year,' he said. Then he hitched up his rucksack and strode away across the ice, his long, gangling frame easy and relaxed. I began shepherding my glacier party. The day's work was just a shade distracted by a wishful anticipation of mountain expeditions on which I would partner this amiable new acquaintance.

By the following winter climbing season, with the Mount Cook territory still absorbing our interest, Geoffrey and I felt ourselves to be competent enough for bigger and better things than the modest exploring we had thus far achieved.

Our target lay in the northern corner of South Island. We planned to explore and make the first winter ascent of Mount Alarm (9,400). With us on the journey went Ian Mackersey, a young reporter, and Theo Hills, another teacher.

Exactly one month before our venture, Hillary with his brother Rex and a friend attempted Mount Alarm, but turned back. Instead they traversed the celebrated 'Tappy' (the 9,465-foot Tapuaenuku) and achieved the second winter ascent of that mountain. In due time we tackled Mount Alarm, reached the summit and on the next day, hugely exhilarated, completed *our* ascent of 'Tappy'.

For those who are unfamiliar with New Zealand conditions it should be noted that some of these mountains are extremely difficult. Altitude alone does not make the mountain, and in fact 10,000 feet around Mount Cook or Mount Alarm is roughly the equivalent of the 14,000-foot Matterhorn in Switzerland, or the 20,000-foot peaks of the Himalayas, where the snow line begins a good deal higher than in New Zealand's mountain areas.

During the next two seasons I was meeting Ed Hillary quite often, though not until 1951 was our plan for a climb realized —and then it was the result of a dreamy speculation while we were incarcerated in a mountain hut, a year earlier, cut off from the world by a violent storm. We had gone, Geoffrey and I, to the hut called Haast which lies on the lower slopes from which the attempt on Mount Cook is made. We reached Haast about the same time as Hillary and his companion, a donnish young man named Bruce Morton.

Then the storm broke and there was nothing for it but to sit tight and hope for the best. Lounging around the hut, the four of us decided to team up for the climb if and when the weather cleared. But the snow streamed down and blew incessantly, and we were besieged for nearly five days. For a time we amused ourselves playing draughts with a board drawn on a large cardboard calendar, our draughtsmen fashioned from chunks of parsnip and carrot. Between desultory games and primitive cooking we daydreamed about the potential joys of climbing in the Himalayas, which in those days was still a distant if not unattainable Mecca for comparatively inexperienced climbers. By the end of the second day our talk was soaring to a more daring level as Hillary and I asked each other, 'Why *not* the Himalayas?'

The fact was that New Zealand mountain training fitted a man more appropriately for a Himalayan expedition than any testing ground in the Swiss Alps. The structure of South Island terrain, with its high plateau country in the east and its deep-cut valleys in the west, was not so dissimilar from the Everest region, and many of our problems were strikingly similar; we carried heavy loads, we had ice rather than rock difficulties, we had no comfortable railways to help the initial stages of ascent, and we had few Alpine amenities; with the planning of food, stores, bases and routes, our New Zealand climbs were 'expeditions' in the proper sense.

And so, around the Christmas of 1950 and into the New Year, I set off on a South Island summer journey deliberately designed with the problems of the Himalayas in our minds. My four companions were Earle Riddiford, a barrister, Bill Beavan, an engineer, Edmund Cotter, a clothing salesman, and Hillary.

Most of our pre-expedition planning was done by letters, for we were separated in various parts of New Zealand until Christmas Eve when we made our mountain rendezvous in a hut on the eastern side of Elie de Beaumont, the most northerly of the country's 10,000-foot peaks, and our newest goal.

Of all the mountains I have seen or perhaps ever will see, Elie de Beaumont has most of the kind of majesty that can be properly called awesome. It is 'big' and difficult, with a long jagged ridge that plunges dramatically down into tangled forests a few miles from the sea. For a mountain of only 10,000 feet it offers the difficulties, resistance, perils and beauty of anything to be found in the Himalayas. High-angled glaciers, hard as diamonds, are draped in every mountain fold with an extravagance that no *couturier* has yet displayed. With its rivers, forests and contorted geography it was a triumph to reach even the foot of Elie de Beaumont, a seven-day trek in the blazing December sunshine, negotiating three uncrossed passes before starting our real assault.

Over the high passes we were each humping loads of seventy pounds, and in some steep sectors it meant double or triple journeys, carrying twenty to thirty pounds at a time—five thoughtful ants toiling hour after hour, climbing day by day, placing our loads on ever higher ledges.

Christmas Day was distinguished only by the dozen or so balloons with which Ed Cotter decorated our camp.

On New Year's Day we were in position to make an attempt on the great ridge. Ed Hillary, who at this stage was not as toughened as he was soon to become, had a tendency to labour at the rear, usually just behind me. His progress in leadership, however, was given an unexpected forward thrust during the

13

morning when we were half-way up the ridge. A sudden storm, blowing in from the sea, forced us to retreat. It was early in the morning, just before dawn, nobody was inclined to talk much, and I was leading, with Ed close behind, head down and panting a little with the effort to keep up.

With my pack pressing hard, I stepped on a small boulder that proved to be unfirm. Overbalancing, I began to fall, quickly recovered, and then stumbled a yard backwards and downwards until a loud agonized yell from Ed indicated that the power-packed heel of my climbing boot had landed with cruel exactitude across his toes.

'The climb is bloody difficult enough without *that*,' said Ed, ruefully examining his bruised foot. 'Next time I'll lead.'

While in the mountains we were often troubled by a parrot called the kea—a colourful, naughty, thieving bird with a destructive beak. The keas are found only in New Zealand. One day Ed, at his unselfconscious and hilarious best, announced his determination to shoot one of these creatures and bring it back for supper.

'Shoot—with what?' I inquired.

'I thought of making a bow and arrow,' Ed said. He then went to work with his ice-axe, cutting a sizeable shaft from a thicket, tied a pair of bootlaces together and eventually fashioned a massive if somewhat unorthodox bow. From the thicket he also hacked a few straight sticks for arrows, built a camp-fire and proceeded to harden the arrow tips in the blaze.

I watched as he sat crouched over the fire, a wild, untidy cave dweller with shaggy hair.

'You look like prehistoric man,' I told him, 'but with rather less chance of making a kill using *that* instrument.'

Hillary rose, stretched his long arms and legs, made a 'prehistoric' grimace, and walked off with his new weapons. I saw him creeping around some rocks, absorbed as any schoolboy playing Red Indians.

14

To the astonishment of all of us, he returned in half an hour triumphantly brandishing a kea.

With all their feathers, they were quite big. Plucked, they were diminutive. We cooked the poor thing in our pressure cooker and each had an inadequate, indigestible mouthful.

A different brand of surprise faced us the next day. From the outset Bill Beavan had complained that he was far from on top of his form, and there was no doubt he was sickening for something by the time we began camping under a large overhanging rock. About the third of the month we were planning to set off before dawn on the main climb to the summit, and it was over breakfast at one o'clock that morning (a vast meal which had to suffice for the whole day) when Bill became obviously ill.

Ed and I first noticed the spots on his face. Bill ripped open his shirt and we saw a still more spotted chest. Bill Beavan had unaccountably caught chicken-pox.

'Leave me a couple of days' food and water,' said Bill quixotically, 'and I'll be all right here under the rock while you finish the climb.'

A nagging suspicion of mean-spiritedness troubled the rest of us for a while, but was soon submerged, I fear, with the prospect of completing the most exciting ascent we had done so far. Hoping for a gallant refusal from Bill, we offered to stay with him, and were relieved when he firmly insisted the expedition must continue.

So we made him as comfortable as possible under the rock and set off.

I climbed with Ed Hillary on my rope, with Earle and Ed Cotter together on a rope behind us. We were on the Maximilian ridge, a jagged highway that could be seen in profile at various points, and, like all first ascents, was full of interesting problems. It meant non-stop climbing for thirteen hours, with no further food and drink after our giant breakfast during the small hours.

The marathon ended between three and four in the afternoon. We reached the summit and looked across at Mount Cook and down on a magnificent panorama of the places across which we had trekked seven days earlier. It was true that this peak had been reached by others before us, but only from the other side of the mountain where the going was much easier. The territory we covered was virtually unknown, with the ice folds and new glaciers to test our skills and confidence. On a new mountain, or a new ridge, every ascent is endlessly fascinating—the climbers never certain what lies on the other side of a rock face, never knowing if they are soon to be forced into retreat; intense concentration, without waste of words, on the slow, slow climb that often reminds you of the tensions in driving a very fast car—there is nothing to discuss, plenty to do, continually learning to adjust yourself.

You climb, you emerge at the top of an ice slope, you bring up your second man on the rope, you cut steps, finger the rocks, and nimbly climb again; every now and then there is an excited shout of relief or triumph; you are afraid, the man behind is also afraid, and you each know about the other but you do not think about it, and you say nothing.

There was little time for resting at the summit, for it was essential to get off the mountain before dark; too dangerous to remain without protection if a storm should blow up. Now, however, a new problem loomed. For several hours Ed's usual exuberance had been noticeably dimmed. By the time we reached the top of the ridge he announced he was not feeling well.

'If you will keep plugging on in front,' he said, 'I can still follow.' And thus we completed the journey to the summit.

The descent was not easy, and by the time we were down, with darkness almost upon us, Ed Hillary was in a feverish condition. He too had chicken-pox.

It was an invaluable expedition despite the setbacks of ill-health. Less than five months later, four of us were on our way for the first time to the magic Himalayas. Fitter than at any time in my life, I thought with amusement about the old prophecy that with my abnormal left arm I was destined to be a partial cripple, physically 'not much use'.

The party consisted of Earle Riddiford, Edmund Cotter, Hillary, and me, and we needed about £1,200 to £1,300 for the four months' expedition. We were known as the New Zealand Garhwal Expedition. My entire savings at this time totalled £150, but Hillary was putting £400 into the kitty, and with help from the New Zealand Alpine Club and the Canterbury Mountaineering Club, and by borrowing an extra hundred or so, I calculated it would be possible to scrape along until September.

I will not go into the daily detail of these climbs, which, although they exceeded our wildest hopes, were mainly significant for the—to us—dynamic outcome.

We began with small ambitions, setting out to explore one of the 20,000-foot peaks of the Indian–Tibetan border. We had been told that if we succeeded with a single mountain of this height the expedition could be counted satisfactory. By the end of August, however, we were a quartet of highly elated climbers, having achieved with the portering aid of four Sherpas not merely the summit of Mukut Parbat (23,760) but also five other mountains exceeding 20,000 feet. Mukut Parbat was then, I believe, the fifteenth highest mountain to have been climbed, though I did not learn that fact until some years later when a German characteristically produced a volume listing all the mountains ever negotiated.

On the way out of the Himalayas we returned to the village of Rhaniket, an old hill station, our expedition base. We were a happy group, ready to sail home and sink ourselves into the comparative modesty of New Zealand's mountains.

At Rhaniket's small hotel we collected our mail, a sizeable batch of letters to be scanned before a good dinner.

And in this parcel of correspondence was a flimsy envelope, formally addressed to the New Zealand Garhwal Expedition.

17

It was a telegram—from the celebrated British mountaineer Eric Shipton—which turned four amiable New Zealanders, relaxing in the hill station lounge, into four tense tigers, caged, self-seeking, eyeing each other with jealousy.

Shipton with a group of British climbers was then about to explore the south side of Everest. He was aware that our New Zealand party had met with success in the Himalayas and his telegram said, in more or less these words:

Invite any two of you to join my party if you can get own permission enter Nepal, bringing own food and supplies.

Any two of us. Wonderful. The chance of a lifetime. Shipton stood high indeed in our estimation. It was like getting a telegram from mountaineering's Angel Gabriel.

Any two of us . . . but which two? Shipton would have gasped if he could have observed the immediate effect of his offer. Into a quiet sitting-room of a mountain hotel he had thrown a hand grenade—not killing anybody but blasting our emotions, churning us collectively and individually, and transforming us above all into a set of stony egotists.

We sat up for hours, long past midnight, arguing and battling for position. Up to this point we had worked and climbed—as New Zealanders often do—without an acknowledged leader, a good co-operative team. Earle Riddiford, however, had done a lot of the initial planning, at which he was most efficient, and it was Earle who read the contents of Shipton's telegram.

We were all shaken by Earle's first words. 'Well, *I* shall be going,' he said coolly, 'and I will decide by the morning who will go with me.'

I burned in silence as he spoke. The truth was that the real tussle lay between Earle and me. Ed Cotter would dearly love to have gone, but he soon retired from the controversy with more or less grace, knowing anyway that he did not possess the extra essential cash to spend several additional weeks in the Himalayas. For that matter I was also broke, but without knowing or caring where the money might come from I was violently possessed by the conviction that I had a moral 'right' to be considered on grounds of fitness alone.

Hillary was a natural choice for two reasons—he could afford the extended trip, and he was now powerfully fit. Earle could certainly afford it, though he was probably in lesser physical condition than I was, or at any rate I thought so. The battle continued. Two, three, four o'clock in the morning came and went. Eventually we retired to bed, but no one slept a wink.

In the end it was settled that Riddiford and Hillary should take advantage of the opportunity. Ed Cotter and I were riddled with envy, flatness and disappointment.

We watched the two set off on their journey to the border where they would pick up their supplies. When they were out of sight we returned to our rooms, dejected, packed our bags and rucksacks, and went to board the train for Bombay. From there we sailed home to New Zealand, still a joyless couple.

Thanks to Ed Hillary, my own opportunity came one year later. On his recommendation I was invited to join the British expedition to climb Cho Oyu (26,850), the formidable next-door neighbour to Everest.

There were ten of us on Cho Oyu that year, and the venture was a tough rehearsal for the Everest expedition of the following summer.

Of these ten, five men were eventually selected for the 1953 assault on Everest. Of the five, two were New Zealanders. Hillary—and, I thanked my lucky stars, me. As an amateur photographer of average enthusiasm I was not then expecting to assume the role of an Everest cameraman.

CHAPTER III

Easy Day for a Lady

I MADE no secret of my amateur status as a photographer. During my climbs at home or abroad I enjoyed taking pictures, grew interested enough to do my own processing, and in terms of keenness and competence was content to remain in the 'good amateur' category, concentrating on black and white stills, without experience or much enthusiasm for the more high-falutin' pleasures of the ciné camera.

It was our successful 1953 Everest Expedition which created a minor myth about my prowess, and within two more years I was to be assigned as official photographer to the Trans-Antarctic party; in the space between the two explorations I seemed to have graduated through an almost accidental apprenticeship into a new profession.

On Everest we were a party of thirteen men not counting the army of Sherpas. Under the leadership of the inspiring John Hunt there were ten climbers, of whom I was one, and three people with specialized duties, a doctor, a physiologist, and Tom Stobart the ciné cameraman.

A marked feature of all the big Himalayan ventures was that the filming invariably petered out and came to a halt before the real business of ascent took place. Almost every group succeeded in making a beautiful picture of the approach, with a variety of pleasant bits and pieces shot on the lower slopes of their mountain; but whenever the true pressure was on—and this applied especially to the Everest problems—everything, including photography and photographers, was sacrificed to the prime task of climbing the mountain.

Our job was to put two men safely on the summit of Everest for the first time in history, and to get them there under conditions where every ounce of weight, every breath of oxygen, every step and every movement of a limb, was a human factor of perpetual importance.

Unluckily for Tom Stobart, he caught a mild dose of pneumonia into the bargain, so it was soon made plain that any photographic achievements higher than 20,000 feet would have to be performed, if at all, by one or other of our mountaineers.

At the beginning Tom had hoped for porters to carry his equipment, which included five or six cameras, and oxygen facilities for himself at the higher altitudes; but it was a vain hope, for by the time we went into the ice-fall, the first big section of the climb, there was certainly no chance for an inessential mountaineer to be prancing around with cameras recording the activity of the rest of us. The ice-fall, no place to dally, was a dangerous, difficult climb demanding all our skills and concentration. Already, at 20,000 feet, it began to look as if photography was out of the running despite the pictorial importance of the climbing job. Tom was understandably dispirited.

Soon we were pushing still higher, a spearhead into the Western Cwm. The role of those lower down was to fix the route, putting in pegs and ropes, bringing up supplies, generally reducing the strain on those of us who were subjected to the greatest degree of tension on the mountain. Realizing he would miss these vital stages without help, Tom asked John Hunt if one or more of the climbers could also make an effort with the cameras. I think he hoped that four climbers might each take a camera, but as things turned out I was the only one to show much interest. Several days earlier, in fact, I had been playing

21

office boy to Tom's directorship, helping to reload his cameras, writing down picture data, studying his technique—and for ever inquiring what he aimed for, what kind of exposures he used for this and that, how he proposed to make the picture whenever he fired a shot.

Then, when the time came to take over some of his equipment, I told him: 'Give me a few elementary instructions and I'll do my best to carry them out.' Stobart at once produced two good unwritten laws in which he firmly believed.

'First, make sure you use a tripod,' he said, 'for every possible picture occasion—otherwise your film will have so much "shake" it will be quite hopeless for big screens. On the other hand,' he added, 'if there's any really exciting action in front of your eyes, don't worry about camera "shake", don't worry about exposures, don't worry a damn about anything . . . just point the camera and shoot. Provided the stuff is dramatic enough, audiences will accept any amount of technical fault.'

All the same, the prospects for successful filming were not particularly bright, notwithstanding my lack of experience. Stobart had long ago discovered, in the photographic 'cold chamber' in London, that the movie camera just would not operate efficiently, or indeed at all, at extremely low temperatures.

We agreed that a hope-for-the-best policy was the most encouragement we could give ourselves, and off I went with two cameras. One was my own Retina II, loaded with colour film (Kodachrome). The other was one of Tom's four small movie cameras, also loaded with colour—an ordinary auto-load Bell-Howell machine with a single lens, of the type used by millions of other amateurs the world over. I kept both cameras tied with cord slung around my neck, day and night.

The weight problem grew worse as we climbed higher. My first groping efforts (it was the first time in my life I'd held a ciné camera) were carried out on the ice-fall. By the time we were into the Western Cwm, and later still on the Lhotse face where for ten days I was leading the spearhead of the climb, and yet again on the South Col towards the summit, I began to appreciate the exact physical significance of every extra ounce.

The movie camera alone weighed four pounds. Each magazine of film added eight more ounces, and I was usually carrying ten magazines at a time. Our normal mountain load for each climber was thirty to fifty pounds, though even on the South Col I found it possible, if wearisome, to handle fifty-five pounds including the camera equipment. There was no need for any fanciful photographic effort on my part. The climbing of Everest is its own spectacle, and I took simple shots of Sherpas and mountaineers at their various tasks, trying all the time to make my twofold record—men in the act of climbing, and the whole process of conquering the mountain. I did not wait long before temperature troubles arrived. The movie camera began running slower and slower until it threatened to stop altogether.

Then I discovered the secret of making it work even in the worst of our icy surroundings.

As every enthusiast knows, there is a small button on the side of the camera case which provides for the setting of the shutter, 16, 24, 32 and up to 64 frames per second—and very soon I became fairly adept at judging the correct speed by the noise, the actual note, the camera made. One day, nearing the Lhotse face, I was convinced the thing was running slow.

I decided to take a chance. That same evening I set the shutter to run at 32 frames per second. Later in the expedition I was sometimes using 48—all in order to ensure that the result would somehow come out at 24 frames.

Luckily for me, and for the Everest film, the gamble came off.

Apart from these tricks I did nothing unorthodox except sleep with the camera equipment inside my vest each night to keep it warm. But screwing the button to a higher-than-normal setting was without a doubt the real advantage, for the cold air then slackened off the mechanism to—providentially—its more or less correct speed.

Even the day when this trick failed to work, the film effect was strikingly successful, and is one that hits me afresh whenever I see the Everest film. On the Lhotse face I was fortunate enough to get some really distinctive shots of a Sherpa cutting steps in the ice. Now at this height the effect of the rarefied atmosphere is to slow down all one's bodily actions. Every working act, every movement of leg and arm is slowed. You may *think* you are doing things at normal speed, but the belief is an illusion; it is also the symbol of gravest danger, for with mental and physical processes thus dimmed and the actor unaware of the fact, that is the moment of peril when a slip to death is most likely.

The Sherpa was seen in the film cutting his steps with the fascinating, graceful, yet tense slow motion that is the characteristic feature of an action performed on Everest.

The truth was that I shot the whole of his activity with my shutter set too fast, greatly exaggerating the reality. Back in London while we were being honoured all over town, I occasionally caught myself in a mood of shameless nonchalance when I was congratulated about the quality of this piece of the film.

There was no denying, however, that I was proud of my shooting, and of the percentage of film that was found usable. I felt myself to be a real photographer at last.

* * *

I have often been asked which of the two expeditions (Everest or Antarctica) I enjoyed the more. I find this a difficult question to answer simply as each was so different.

Everest was shorter in time: for three months we concentrated every ounce of energy in forcing upwards to place two people on a single point; the Trans-Antarctic expedition lasted

24

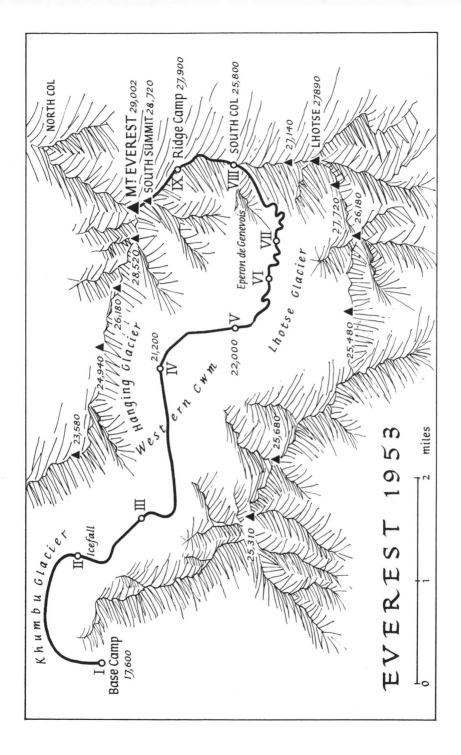

EVEREST 1953

NORTH COL

MT. EVEREST 29,002
SOUTH SUMMIT 28,720
Ridge Camp 27,900
IX
SOUTH COL 25,800
VIII
27,140
LHOTSE 27890

28,520

26,180

27,720

26,180

24,940
Hanging Glacier
Eperon de Genevois
VI VII
25,480

23,580
21,200
IV
V
22,000
Lhotse Glacier

Western Cwm

III
25,680

Icefall
II
25,310

Khumbu Glacier

I
Base Camp
17,600

0   1   2
miles

three years and required a dogged, plodding tenacity, in order that sixteen people might cross a flat, monotonous plain.

The seventeen-day march across the Nepalese valleys to the wall of the Himalayas was one of sharp and delightful contrasts to be found in climbing a mountain. It was springtime as we walked the hundred and seventy miles to the monastery at the foot of Everest; flowering almond trees and rhododendrons bloomed and in the clear mornings the peaks, incredibly high, stood beyond.

Although I had met and climbed with some of the Everest party there were several I was meeting for the first time, but I had heard so much about them that it was like meeting old friends. Wylie and Ward I took to immediately; the others were much quieter. Noyce was rather reserved, slow of speech and, I thought, probably prosaic and undemonstrative (how wrong I was to think him prosaic: he was a poet and anything but a commonplace unromantic man). George Band was the baby of our party—six feet three inches topped by a panama hat, he looked like a dedicated missionary. He was still at Cambridge University and was accounted as the most outstanding of the younger British climbers. The person I knew least about and met last of all was John Hunt. He greeted me most warmly and said how much he was depending on me—his assault on personal susceptibilities was impossible to resist. I was taken aback as I had heard that he was a crisp, machine-like martinet colonel, and when Ed Hillary and I leapt from our tent on the first morning and sloped ice-axes with military precision, our antics fell rather flat.

On the third evening of our march three of us went for a short stroll to watch the clouds rolling over the distant range. Later John Hunt and Michael Westmacott came by with butterfly nets and began chasing butterflies. They were collecting, I think, for a museum: I was amused to watch them stalking up to a thorny shrub with their nets poised: it seemed incongruous that these hardy mountaineers should be such

26

crackpot-looking butterfly-catchers, but before long I too had joined the hunt and was enjoying the fun.

At sunset the clouds over the peaks rolled away and we all ran to see the peaks turn gold in the setting sun. We ate curried rice, tinned steak, boiled potatoes and peas in the big communal tent and then took our sleeping-bags outside and lay identifying the stars and planets.

At the end of the march we reached Thyangboche Monastery, one of the most beautiful sights in all the Himalayas, where we set up camp in a grassy meadow allocated us by the lamas. All around the sanctuary were mountains of the most fantastic shapes. At the head of the valley stood Everest, clear and almost black on one side, and streaming with a plume of snow and cloud on the other. It looked immensely high and formidable.

At Thyangboche we broke into three parties and set off to climb and explore, to get acclimatized to higher altitudes and try an open circuit oxygen test run at eighteen or twenty thousand feet. I went in John Hunt's party with Gregory and Tenzing. Tenzing had been to 28,000 feet with the Swiss attempt on the mountain, and from the beginning he was treated by John Hunt as one of the potential 'summiters'. Our party went up the Imja valley where we explored a glacier and climbed a hidden peak of just under 20,000 feet. From a camp at 18,000 feet we all tried for the first time wearing and using the oxygen sets. A set weighed thirty-five pounds and was comparatively complicated, and I was most interested to see if the advantage of having the oxygen would outweigh the disadvantage of the weight of the equipment. I had walked up to 18,000 feet for the first time and was feeling lethargic with a headache. I did not want in the slightest to push on to 19,800 feet. However, with Tenzing I fitted on the mask and checked the bottles and flow rates, connected up and switched on. We set off together, each adding to our natural intake three litres of oxygen every minute. Instead of puffing and panting I breathed deeply and evenly and stepped up without the feeling of fatigue that one has before being acclimatized. It was a great relief to know the outfit really worked.

With every breath I heard the economizer give a little gasp and send a puff of gas into the mask. The tiny valves in the mask flip-flopped with each breath and I felt wonderful. With the mask and tube and goggled eyes Tenzing looked a rare specimen of the scientific age and I felt I did, too.

Twenty-five minutes later and five hundred feet higher there was a sudden explosion and roaring of air and I nearly fell over with fright. Tenzing was clawing at his frame: his reducing valve had blown out. I closed the tap on his bottle and took off his set and we saw that we could not repair the valve. Tenzing went down and I pushed on.

I soon forgot the incident and began to marvel at the boost that the set was giving me. Whether it was so or not, I don't know, but I had a feeling of power and rhythm with the oxygen flowing. There was a slight hiss from the bottle and the mask kept the cold from my face. Drops of moisture dribbled out of the mask outlet and froze soon after hitting the ground.

The top of the hill looked far away when I stopped to change the flow rate to six litres per minute, and I was amazed to find myself on the rocky summit after ten minutes. On six litres I felt like running and could climb at sea-level pace. I sat down for a minute to drink in the high flow rate and enjoy the view. The return, unaided to conserve oxygen, was not uncomfortable, although I noticed the weight of the set, where before I had not. Hunt and Gregory, and lastly Tenzing, did the same run with good apparatus. We all climbed to 18,000 feet in about an hour—Tenzing actually did it in fifty minutes, which for any altitude is rapid climbing.

Tenzing was very fit; he moved beautifully and was well used to high altitudes. He was unspoiled, although even then he had received considerable publicity because of his climbing. He was a good companion who fitted in with everyone. He had an infectious sense of humour and a desire to yodel and whoop when he was happy. He spoke a few words of English and taught me some Hindustani and a few words of Tibetan. There is in him a natural elegance and a gentle manner; he is not a forthright character, but a dreamer, and after Everest he was bewildered and often unhappy at the complications of fame. He has said, sadly, and I think honestly: 'I wish sometimes that I had never climbed Everest.'

*　　　*　　　*

The assault proper began with four of us tackling a cataract of ice which debauched from the high hanging valley which has been called the Western Cwm. Working in relays, we established a series of camps up the ice-fall and into the Western Cwm, while a party made a higher reconnaissance using the closed circuit oxygen equipment (from which they recoiled with heat exhaustion by over-heating of the soda-lime canisters, which led Charles Evans to remark, 'We know it's possible to reach the South Col *without* oxygen; the purpose of this reconnaissance is to try to reach it *with* oxygen.')

Ed, with Tenzing, arranged an energetic test on open circuit equipment to see if the use of it at lower altitudes gave them any real benefit. On 2nd May they left Base Camp at the crack of dawn to climb to Camp IV. They came back the same afternoon in a great blizzard, tired but certainly not exhausted as one would be without oxygen, and Ed swung off his set and proclaimed it was 'bloody marvellous'.

Their times were:

6.30 from Base 18,000 feet
8.00 at Camp II 19,500 feet
8.50 at Camp III 20,500 feet
10.50 at Camp IV 22,000 feet.

This was a terrific set of times as our normal programme was to go to:

Camp II the first day in 3 hours and rest
Camp III the second day in $2\frac{1}{2}$ hours and rest
Camp IV the third day in $3\frac{1}{2}$ hours and rest.

This outstanding run singled out Ed and Tenzing as the fittest and most energetic pair, and one which obviously went well as a team. Tenzing's performance altogether fitted neatly into John Hunt's ideal—his hope that one of the summit pair would be a Sherpa, that one of the East and one of the West would top the mountain together.

How this hope was realized I was able to describe in one of the series of letters which I wrote home during the three months we spent on Everest:

Base Camp. 1st June 1953.

. . . At present don't imagine our band of thirteen rolling and rollicking in an ecstasy brought on by victory. If you were at Base Camp now you would see nine sahibs and about fifteen Sherpas lying listlessly around the tents with bloodshot and glazed eyes, thin, dirty and bewildered. Ed now is sleeping as he has done for hours and hours, Charles is just smoking and tired; the talk is very desultory and dull; everyone is quite played out. Five of the other lads will be descending tomorrow from Camp III and they too will come in stiff-legged and flogged after the last two weeks.

Two days ago we were on the South Col urging ourselves to the limit—and now like pricked balloons all our reserves have gone. Yesterday we came down to Base Camp. Ed, Charles Evans and I were together on one rope and it took hours. I have never been so tired, nor had Ed. Now, if you could see us, you would see the most beaten, played-out, lustreless team of climbers that it is possible to imagine.

When the great lift reached the South Col on the 22nd May, John Hunt decided to launch the Assault Plan and accordingly the closed circuit boys went into action. Tom Bourdillon and Charles Evans set off on the afternoon of the 22nd with all their

30

bedding tied around their closed circuit apparatus, with spare soda-lime canisters and spanners poking out—in all some 50 lbs. John Hunt went with them on open circuit as support and possible emergency. Two Sherpas also went (Da Namgyl and Balu, who had been specially chosen) to carry a tent and oxygen above the South Col as a possible emergency ration and shelter in the case of a late descent by Tom and Charles. In the event of this tent and oxygen not being used it was to be added to by the second assault party (Ed and Tenzing) backed by Gregory and three special Sherpas, who would establish Ridge Camp— Camp IX.

It was at this stage that I came into the story. The original plan did not include me but I was very keen to get to South Col. Because of Ed and Tenzing's trip to South Col with the first Sherpa lift and their consequent tiredness, they decided to wait a day longer than originally planned. Then it was discovered, mostly by my propaganda, that a little more oxygen and food would be advisable. Accordingly I was commissioned to escort five Sherpas to South Col along with Gregory and his three special Ridge Camp boys to back up Ed and Tenzing. I spent all 23rd May frantically trying to fix a leak in the oxygen set I was to use. Finally by cutting and binding one of the rubber feed pipes I stopped the hiss. Tom, Charles and John climbed to Camp VII on the 23rd.

24th May. Tom, Charles and John with their two Sherpas crept above Camp VII and worked slowly to South Col. We watched them through glasses; they were slow, seven hours, and arrived late and very tired. We packed up and Greg and I with our Sherpas left for Camp V, where we spent the night (a cold night—our thermometer read —27° Centigrade at 5 a.m.).

25th May. Tom and Charles were timed to make an attempt on the South Peak—and summit if possible, using closed circuit. Due to weather (wind) and their tired condition from previous day they stayed on South Col. Greg and I left for VI using oxygen (two litres per minute). We made good time, and at VI I changed to four litres and we headed on up the Lhotse face for VII. You will remember that the climb from V to VII is up the difficult Lhotse face on which nearly a thousand feet of rope is fixed. Above VI I began to falter. I began to pant and weaken although Greg was making a slow pace. I began to worry and think I was failing—but it turned out to be a defect in my oxygen set which was cutting right out and the mask was stopping even the outside air getting in. The trip to VII, for me, was hell, and I collapsed on the snow there and took a couple of hours to recover. At VII I was able to trace the trouble and the set behaved beautifully the next day. Ed and Tenzing came right through to VII from IV that day and arrived fresh and fit.

Although Everest was blowing a cloud plume on these days the weather was very settled and the weather report (from Indian radio) gave us: 'Warm temperatures, winds 15–20 knots and settled weather. Monsoon still only in the Andaman Sea.' Camp VII (24,000 feet approximately) was calm that night (Temp. —28° Centigrade).

26th May. We left VII at 8.45 a.m. and had wonderful conditions for our climb to South Col. I filmed much of the climb and felt really wonderful. The climb starts near the top of the Lhotse face glacier and for perhaps a thousand feet is a steady crampon climb up crevassed slopes and then swings left to traverse above rock bands and goes diagonally and up the great snow slopes towards the Col. The South Col is not reached direct. The rock buttress of 'Eperon de Genevois' stops this and our route connected with the very top of the Eperon over which we climbed and dropped several hundred feet into the South Col (25,850 feet).

About 1 p.m. on 26th we began traversing rock and snow at the top of the Eperon. The South Peak of Everest was in view (the South Peak is a beautiful snow peak and sweeps up looking incredibly steep) and on the final slope I saw two dots, like

Elie de Beaumont, in New Zealand's Southern Alps

Top right: Ed Hillary at a camp in Tibet during the 1952 Cho Oyu Expedition. The peak beyond is Cho Rapzang

Bottom right: Ed on the summit of a 21,000-foot peak during the 1952 Expedition

Below: I help Ed Cotter in a crossing of a New Zealand river

John Hunt leads a party of Sherpas up the ice-fall on Everest

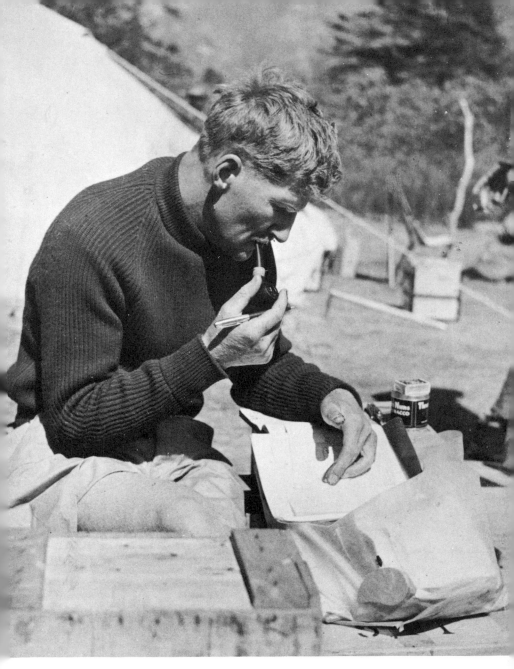

John Hunt

Left : Makalu, 27,790 feet

Right : John Hunt, Ed Hillary, Tenzing, Ang Nima, Alf Gregory and me on 30th May 1953, the day after the summit of Everest had been reached

Right : Everest, photographed by the Indian Air Force six days after the climb. The South Col is the snow saddle to the right of the summit

Return to the Himalayas after the American lecture tour: Charles Evans, myself, and Ed Hillary

flies on a wall, about two hundred feet below the cornice of the top. We went mad with excitement as we watched Tom and Charles go steadily up and over the South Summit (28,720 feet) and, we thought, off for the main summit. They were higher than anyone had ever been before and were apparently going at a very fast rate. They had climbed from the South Col that morning and reached the South Summit in five and a half hours. John too had set out with Da Namgyl (both on open circuit) ahead of Tom and Charles to carry Ridge Camp, but with closed circuit they easily overtook him and far outclassed the open circuit at the highest altitudes. Balu, the other Sherpa, had not gone above South Col.

Greg and I were so excited at seeing Tom and Charles that we ran down into the Col Camp to shout the news to Ed and Tenzing. Ed came out of the dome tent with a great whoop and then dived back again. Tenzing, we were hurt to find, lost his smile and did not share our enthusiasm. The idea of team effort had not been revealed to him, and the idea that anybody but Tenzing should reach the summit was not pleasurable to him.

Ed's disappearance into the dome I thought strange, and I pushed my way in to find John lying quite exhausted with Ed plying drinks and oxygen. Ed and Tenzing had arrived on the Col before us and Ed saw John returning with Da Namgyl from his ridge carry. John and Da Namgyl had carried to 27,350 feet, and were returning completely done in. John was staggering and crumpling and staggering on again, when Ed rushed off to help him. Ed assisted him on his shoulder and slapped his oxygen mask on him for a good half-hour (John's oxygen had run out at 27,350 and he came down without). Da Namgyl's hands were frost-bitten and he was very tired.

John certainly earned our admiration—he's got tremendous guts and this day he pushed himself to the absolute limit—but this was typical of him all through.

There were three tents on South Col; a pyramid, a dome and a Meade. They respectively housed four, two and two. The

33

pyramid had previously been used by Sherpas and was in a disgraceful condition. The floor was in shreds and parting at the stitching at the seams. The windward side had a four-inch tear which later caused great inconvenience by admitting drifting snow and cold wind. The rope guys were far too tight and in the tremendous and ceaseless buffeting on the Col they were fraying and broken when we arrived. Ed and I went out in the afternoon into a freezing, roaring wind and began to repair the tent. We found a pile of strong Swiss line and began replacing all the guys and placing rocks around the worst tears in the floor to protect it from the plucking of the wind.

During this time the South Summit became enveloped in cloud and we began to worry about Tom and Charles. We knew, as they knew, that if their closed circuit sets failed in any way (and they had many gadgets, valves, tubes and canisters susceptible to error) they would not come back. Tom was an exceedingly determined thruster and we felt his enthusiasm could overcome good sense—but Ed remarked, 'Charles is pretty sensible—I think he'll balance Tom.'

About this time the three Sherpas who had been chosen to carry with Greg to the Ridge Camp arrived on the Col from Camp VII. They had set out with us and gone slowly and badly. This was disturbing as we had placed high hopes on them. They were Ang Temba, Pemba and Ang Nima. Ang Temba we thought the best and were amazed to find that when he dumped his load (30 lbs.) outside the tent he keeled over and for ten minutes was out cold. Pemba was very tired, while Ang Nima was quite fresh and unaffected by the altitude.

John by this time had recovered and was fretting about for Tom and Charles. He kept peering up the ridge looking for their return. The afternoon passed and we all became more and more worried. As we fixed the last ropes I saw some moving dots at the head of the couloir by which they had reached the ridge. I watched until in the shifting mist I was certain and shouted the news. Our relief was tremendous.

34

Their descent of the couloir was frightening to watch. Dog tired, they started down one at a time, each anchoring the other and each falling off as they tried to kick downhill. They slid and fell, their rope lengths each just managing to hold the other. As Tom said, 'We yo-yo'd our way down—it was quite fun!'

Ed and I went out to meet them and I filmed their arrival. They were still wearing and using their closed circuit, and apart from the masks which covered nose, mouth and chin, they were covered in icicles. Ice driblets from the mask outlet had stuck to their windproofs and they were panting and labouring just to move along the flat.

They had not gone far beyond the South Summit—a few yards only—their soda-lime canisters did not leave them with enough time in hand to risk going on. The Summit Ridge seemed long (Tom judged two or three hours and Charles thought four or more), it was corniced and had a difficult vertical rock step in it. Tom took eighteen photographs and they turned down. Just below the South Summit they jettisoned two oxygen bottles, having enough left to get to South Col. These bottles were a vital help in getting Ed and Tenzing to the top two days later.

That night Ed, Tenzing, Greg and I slept in the pyramid, while Ang Temba, Pemba and Ang Nima passed the night in the even smaller dome. That night for everyone was pure misery. The wind slammed over the Col and worried the tents, whining, roaring and snapping incessantly. It became the curse of the Col, sapping our tempers and eating indelibly into our memories. We will never forget the South Col. We all spent there the most miserable days and nights of our lives.

The temperature dropped until we were all cold even though fully dressed (we wore our high-altitude boots in the sleeping-bag to stop them freezing) with full down clothing and our warm sleeping-bags. I have never been so miserable with freezing feet (they were lightly frost-bitten—getting better now), cold knees and back which was rammed hard against the windward side of the tent. My pillow was a kitbag full of frozen snow—hard, cold, and unsatisfactory. What a night! But it was only the first of four which grew increasingly worse.

At 4.30 a.m. we began to prepare breakfast in the hope of an early start in carrying Ridge Camp. Our appetites were good—we had carried up some 'luxury food' and ate the lot at breakfast. I remember the menu—'Vita-Wheat' biscuits with honey; sardines on biscuit ('Vita-Wheat'); two tins of pineapple (between four); slices of saucisson (salami or raw bacon sausage); biscuits and honey, and lastly a tin of Australian pears. We ate and spread honey with gloves on and you can imagine what a messy business it was.

Our hopes of starting faded when at 8 a.m. the wind velocity had increased to over 70 or 80 m.p.h. and never looked like decreasing. All day, 27th May, it blew and put the chances of climbing on a ridge out of the question.

Supplies on the Col were limited and Charles and Tom had to go down. Ang Temba was so sick that he too was to go down. John, too, although he felt as leader he should stay to see and support the main assault, decided to go down and leave me to join the Ridge Camp carry. With Ang Temba out of the carry, someone had to replace him and I was fit. So again, although not supposed in the plan to stay on South Col, I was now in the Ridge party.

Ang Temba, Tom, Charles and John left in the howling wind. Their climb to the top of the Eperon (three hundred feet) took nearly two hours. Ed and I assisted them—they were dreadfully weak but once over the Eperon they were out of the worst wind and going downhill. Their journey to VII was an epic and there they were received by Wilfrid Noyce and Mike Ward. On the 28th they limped to Advance Base, to good food, attention and rest.

For the remainder of 27th May we sat out the wind and dreaded the coming of night. The night was a repetition of the previous one and in the morning we were still bad-tempered and ill-fed with very frayed morale. The wind mercifully eased and we stiffly prepared to go. Three hours it took to make a few simple preparations. Then an apparently crippling blow fell. Pemba suddenly spewed over the tent floor and began to groan and said he couldn't go. That left one Sherpa, Ang Nima, and we needed three. That hour the expedition hopes recorded their lowest reading!

After a discussion we agreed to try and lift the two extra Sherpa loads between us. The weights were about 45 lbs., each of which seemed Herculean when a good load *at this altitude* was considered to be 15 lbs.

Greg, Ang Nima and I got away at 8.45 a.m. Ed and Tenzing decided to delay at least an hour to save their strength and oxygen while we cut steps up the couloir. We were heavily clothed and with the loads we stomped along like robots. We made a very slow steady pace which we managed to hold without stopping, and began to make height. The wind dropped to a comparative breeze and we slugged up into the couloir and I began cutting steps. Cutting steps at 27,000 is an experience— a study in 'go slow'. It took three hours to get up to the ridge (27,200 feet) where we saw the wreckage of the Swiss top camp (one tent) with not a vestige of the cloth on the aluminium bones. Here we dropped our loads and enjoyed the tremendous view. Lhotse and Makalu were wonderful, Kangchenjunga jutted out above the clouds. Below was the Kangshung and Kharta glaciers, with wonderful views of brown Tibet beyond. Oddly enough I enjoyed and remembered the couloir climb and the view as if it were at sea-level. I had read that altitude robbed both enjoyment and memory. With me it was not so. Here Ed and Tenzing caught up with us. Greg was going exceedingly well, Ang Nima the same, and we urged him on by saying that if he went a bit higher he would have carried and gone higher than any Sherpa in the world. He was very ambitious and carried magnificently. About a hundred and fifty feet above here we reached John's highest point and found the rolled tent, food, an R.A.F. oxygen cylinder and other oddments, and these we had to add to our loads. Ed took the tent, Greg the R.A.F. cylinder, and I took food oddments and some of Greg's load: we left there with Ed carrying 63 lbs.; Greg 50 lbs.; self 50 lbs.; Ang Nima 45 lbs.; and Tenzing 43 lbs.

From here the ridge is moderately steep—odd broken rock and towers followed by snow ridge. I led and the snow was bloody—knee deep and loose. From then on the upward progress was grim dead-brained toil. I don't really know how we endured the weight. We pushed up to where we thought a flat spot would be and found it quite untenable. We pushed on again—and again the same thing—and so on. At about 2.30 p.m. we stopped below a snow shoulder and found a tiny ledge where we dumped our loads. Ed and Tenzing began clearing a site which was too small for the tent. Snow flurries were beginning, and although very tired we set off within two minutes of arrival after some cheery banter to and from Ed on the chances for the morrow. The height of Camp IX—Ridge Camp—has been estimated at 27,900 feet.

Our return was slow and tough. Greg had cracked up, Ang Nima was very tired and I had to recut steps all the way down the couloir. From the couloir Greg was collapsing every fifty yards and gasping with exhaustion. I was tired—dreadfully tired but quite able to keep going without pause—and funnily enough with sufficient mentality to appreciate the glorious evening colours over Kangchenjunga and Makalu. I photographed them. Near the tents I unroped and pushed on. Pemba had made a hot drink and I tossed this down, grabbed the movie camera, staggered out and, sitting against a rock, filmed the arrival of Greg and Ang Nima, which I hope shows something of the state of really flogged men. We drank hot lemon and tea and crawled into our bags—but not to sleep. The night, the wind and the cold came and we passed another bloody night. Bloodiest for Greg because he spent an agonizing

38

hour and a half groaning and straining in the darkness of our tent trying to get his bowels to function. Outside on the Col was so miserable and the desire caught him soon after dozing off. He was so constipated and so exhausted that he couldn't manage his task and he knelt groaning and straining over an old tin at my feet. I was too tired to care and just lay careless of his deep trouble. He remembers it as his most terrible experience.

The 29th May finally dawned. On the Col it was windy—it was always windy. The sun hit the top of the tent about 5 a.m. It crept down the walls, releasing the frost of condensed breath in a shower over us—as usual. At 8 a.m. we saw Ed and Tenzing on the way up the final slopes of the South Summit— going slowly but steadily. Greg had decided to go down as he was too weak to be of use to any returning summit party. Ang Nima and Pemba went down too and left me alone on the Col to receive Ed and Tenzing. At 9 a.m. they disappeared over the South Peak and somehow then I felt that they would reach the summit. I boiled soup and lemonade and filled the two Thermos flasks we had. I prepared oxygen bottles with all connections and masks ready for instant use and set bedding ready as if to receive casualties.

Outside I prepared the spare oxygen frame with the two emergency cylinders which I intended to carry up and meet them to assist their descent.

At 1 p.m. they appeared again on South Summit and began the descent of the steep loose snow slope. I was wildly excited and leapt into action. I packed the Thermos flasks, slung the movie camera in (4 lbs.)—put on crampons, gloves—greased my nose, face and lips against the wind—tied a scarf round my face for extra protection (I was severely windburnt and my skin was frost-affected from the other days—and very sore); got into the oxygen-carrying frame with two bottles and set off to meet the boys. About four hundred yards from camp I began to feel groggy—I was carrying too much, had started too excited

39

and too fast, and was climbing without inhaling oxygen. After the previous day's effort I was not as good as I thought. I looked up and saw Ed and Tenzing were coming down quite fast and steadily and were so far away that I could be of no immediate help, so I tottered back to the tent. There I watched them from the tent door. They stopped at Camp IX at 2 p.m. and didn't leave there until 3 p.m. (they had a boil up of lemonade and collected their sleeping-bags), and came down the ridge and then the couloir going absolutely steadily.

Just before 4 p.m. I set out again to meet them, and as I left the tents Wilf Noyce arrived with Pasang Phutar. He had been sent up by John as a useful support to receive and help the summit party in case they were exhausted. It was good to see them and they began to prepare hot drinks as I left.

I dragged up again and met Ed and Tenzing at the foot of the couloir—perhaps five hundred feet above the Col. They were moving fairly rapidly—the only tiredness showed in their slightly stiff-legged walking as they cramponed the last bit of the couloir. I crouched, back against the wind, and poured out the Thermos contents as they came up. Ed unclipped his mask and grinned a tired greeting, sat on the ice and said in his matter-of-fact way—'Well, we knocked the bastard off!'

CHAPTER IV

Lecturer's Spring

AFTER Everest came the wining, the dining, the lecture tours. For many months I was to continue spending most of my time in the stimulating company of Ed Hillary, and now too I began to realize what fantastic strides the man had made from mountaineer to potential leader. Until Everest our climbing careers, along with the progress of that basic driving initiative which good climbing demands, were running more or less in step. But Ed strode mightily forward on Everest, in every sense of the term; and a year later he was the natural leader among us for an exploration into another delectable corner of the Himalayas near Everest.

First, however, the wining and dining. It began within minutes of our return to England, and together with our packed diary of lectures lasted a month until we flew home to New Zealand—there to be given a further exhaustive spell of the same treatment.

Life was moving a good deal faster than on any mountain. Ed carried out the proverbial whirlwind courtship, and on the third of September married a girl we both knew: Louise Rose, whose father was president of the New Zealand Alpine Club. At the wedding I was his best man. Twenty-four hours later we were boarding the aircraft for another trip to Europe, followed by a still more heady round of lectures that seemed to span every major or minor city between Reykjavik and Rome. In England, France, Scandinavia, Finland, Belgium, Holland, Italy, we were telling the Everest tale at the rate of twelve to fifteen lectures a week. It was the only time in my life I had ever earned fairly big money.

Towards the end of this hectic year I met for the first time Vivian Fuchs, the so inappropriately-named 'Bunny'. I confess an odd paradox about my recollection of this event. For most people an introduction to Fuchs is an outstanding experience, and a hundred times I have heard how forcefully people were struck by the man, by his eyes and bearing, by the look of determination in the undeniably handsome face, by the aura of personality. As a general rule I too have a good memory for detail—and yet I did not remember Bunny as a human being on this first encounter. I remembered the Antarctic idea, even though I was not then especially drawn to it. I remembered the flat, even tones of a voice that might have come through a studio speaker in another room . . . but not for many months did the man behind the voice emerge.

By the end of January 1954, three of us from the Everest party—Hillary, Charles Evans, the deputy leader, and I— were embarking on two more expeditions. The first, and in a sense the most gruelling, was a two-months, coast-to-coast, how-we-climbed-it, why-we-did-it lecture tour of the United States. The second, still in its birth pangs, was a New Zealand Alpine Club expedition to be carried out in the Himalayan region of Makalu (27,790), the fourth highest mountain, un-climbed, unexplored, and every bit as testing as Everest.

The grand American tour, talking our way up Everest, with Steak Diane for rations, with Cadillacs for Sherpas, with nightly climbs over glassy peaks of Scotch or Bourbon on the rocks— the alcoholic Western Cwm, the dipsomaniac ice-fall—was the worst kind of training programme for our assault on Makalu. What was worse, the junketing did not end in the United States. Ed and I worked our way lecturing down through Honolulu, then across the Pacific to Fiji, finally home again to New Zealand. Four days later we flew to Calcutta, took the train to the Nepalese border (where we again met Charles Evans who had come round the world from the other side), and on the 1st of April we walked wearily into the Himalayas—three fat and flabby climbers suffering from what Dylan Thomas once called 'the ulcerous rigours of a lecturer's Spring'. Getting ourselves back into condition was a process almost as exhausting as the good living which lay behind and inside us.

From America we had brought at least one astringent experience that gave us deep satisfaction. It was an article written by the leader writer of the National Geographical Society, who was assigned to obtain a story from the great Sir Ed Hillary while we were visiting New York. By that time we were all fed to the teeth with newspaper reporters and endless interviews with their unceasing demand for fresh 'anecdote'. Now, even a journalist from such dignified circles as the National Geographic was no longer being given much of a welcome. The writer was an extremely amiable as well as persistent young man, however, and as Hillary expressed it later: 'Only a chap with a fine sense of humour could have withstood the cold war of George Lowe, Charles Evans and myself.'

In the end the man produced a neatly designed piece in the form of *Notes from the Journal of Sherpa Bevsing*. His final paragraphs gave us untold joy . . .

Installed in a drawing-room with Hillary, I encouraged him to stretch out his long, lanky frame, take his boots off, and retell the account of his ascent, foot by sweating foot. For four hours we worked our way back up the mountain. I found, to my delight, that I was now quite well acclimatized: even in the worst sections, where the narrative had been packed down hard and tight by previous parties, I managed to keep my footing, and the drowsiness which afflicts many writers at this stage scarcely bothered me.

Hillary, however, was obviously having a rougher time. His phrases were becoming more and more laboured; his invention seemed to be flagging; at times I found him almost about to yawn, until he caught himself with an effort and moved on. He even complained of a headache —a common enough affliction on this ascent, but one which he has trained himself usually to suppress.

The last ten pages were the critical part. Our notes were coming more and more slowly. At one point I wondered whether we had not better give up altogether and admit failure. After all, the mountain had beaten better teams in its day; there would be no disgrace in turning back. But just then, in a final magnificent burst of New Zealand slang, Hillary lurched forward and achieved the crest. We had made it!

Later, I asked Hillary where he was going to camp in Boston.

'At the Statler,' he replied.

'But why?'

And this was his answer—one which I shall always remember. Quite simply, but with a deep undercurrent of emotion, he said:

'Because it is there.'

CHAPTER V

No Obituary

Our attempt on the great Makalu, which was in the end frustrated and turned into a successful climb of the nearby ice spire Baruntse (23,760) was notable for two major incidents. One was a terrifying combination of frost-bite and crevasse accident, the other a predicament of Hillary's which had the effect of putting even *The Times* into a dither when it learned they possessed no obituary of Sir Edmund.

Under Ed's leadership we were known as the New Zealand Barun Expedition; we were all New Zealanders save for two Englishmen, the doctor Charles Evans and Michael Ball.

We went into the Himalayas near the foot of Makalu and then broke into three exploring parties. The first was headed by Hillary, the second by Charles Evans; the third party was mine. Ed had the more ponderous and less interesting task of establishing our base and doing survey work. Evans and I, blessed with far more exciting and dramatic territory, explored two parallel valleys, then made our way over the high passes and down into a valley at the foot of Makalu which was our rendezvous point, lying at about 18,000 feet.

I reached the rendezvous one evening to find that although the base camp was established, Ed had left a note saying he had gone off with his group exploring the head of the valley. We went to bed.

45

Next morning I looked out of my tent around seven o'clock, and was perturbed to see Hillary—alone and walking unsteadily—approaching a few hundred yards away. Arriving in camp so early in the morning, and alone, was unusual enough, but his lopsided gait made it patently obvious that something was amiss.

I went to meet him. His first words were: 'There's been an accident. Jim Macfarlane went down a crevasse and he's badly frost-bitten. Hands and feet like big lumps of lead—no feeling in them—absolutely solid.'

'But what's wrong with *you*?' I asked.

Ed ignored the question and went on: 'Brian Wilkins also fell, but managed to get out only slightly hurt. He has stayed with Jim while I came to get help.'

Ed, coughing badly, looked very unhappy. 'What's ailing *you*?' I said again. At this point we reached the tent, and eventually I got the full story.

In almost total darkness, two nights earlier, Hillary had gone down into the crevasse on the end of a rope in an unsuccessful effort to extricate Jim Macfarlane. Unable to reach the frost-bitten trapped man, Ed called to the Sherpas, holding the rope on the edge of the crevasse, to pull him out. With the wind howling madly they heard only garbled shouts. But they did pull on the rope, and when he was nearing the top of the crevasse Ed threw his arms above his head to let them know he was there. Encouraged when they saw his waving hands, the Sherpas gave another mighty drag, and as Ed came up, with the rope tightening around his body, he crashed and scraped against the icy edge, doing considerable damage to his ribs (though he thought it was merely a dose of bad bruising).

Early the next day they found Jim still alive, but woefully concussed. In daylight they were able to complete the rescue, and as soon as he was brought to the surface Ed set off down the glacier to fetch help.

He travelled all that day, slept a few hours on the glacier,

46

resumed at dawn—and reached the point where I saw him staggering down the valley at seven o'clock.

What none of us knew until the doctor later examined him was that the resilient Hillary had come through all this with three broken ribs, caused by the scraping and thumping he received while dangling on the end of a rope in the crevasse.

Being Hillary, he was not prepared to cancel our plans. 'Go ahead with the reconnaissance,' he said, 'and I'll catch you up in a few days when I feel fit enough.'

Being Hillary, he also felt fit enough, or so he thought, as soon as his impetuous, unrelaxing high spirits returned.

Much too soon for his own good, he climbed to where we had set up camp at 22,000 feet.

And in the morning, while in the act of putting on his boots, he suddenly fainted.

One hour later he was in a serious condition.

He was also delirious, and unable to recognize anyone in our party except me. All the time he kept asserting that he knew I would be able to help him, and then he'd start rambling . . .

'Keep the sun off the back of my neck. . . . Stop my feet from getting frost-bite. . . . Geoff's dead . . . I know he's dead. . . . My feet are frost-bitten . . .' and so on.

There was nothing for it but to switch our operations to the vital task of getting him to safety and medical care. The trouble was, we had no stretcher—and it was not easy to lumber his big body down over the long ice slopes we had climbed.

At last, however, we got him to the lower camp where the doctor went to work. With oxygen soon being pumped into him, Ed revived a little; but Charles Evans declared it was touch and go. There was something radically wrong with his chest. 'I think he's got pneumonia,' said Charles, 'but the whole thing is complicated because he also shows all the symptoms of malaria as well.'

This was a real puzzle, for of all complaints afflicting Himalayan climbers, malaria is hardly to be expected.

47

Ed, as it happened, had contracted malaria in the Pacific during the war . . . and now it was coming out in this strange fashion under icy mountain conditions of great stress.

Before long, a message went down to civilization saying that Ed was in trouble, and within twenty-four hours the story had ripped through the world's headlines. HILLARY IS SICK . . . with the stories dwelling on the dreaded dangers of pneumonia at high altitudes.

In London (we learned much later) there was consternation. Hillary was dying. The man who had stood on Everest's summit was slowly reaching his end on a mountain not far away.

The Times went into sombre action with a phone call to Sir John Hunt, our Everest leader. They had slipped up, it seemed, and did not possess in their files enough material for Ed's final tribute. Would Sir John be good enough to write Sir Edmund's obituary?

John was truly cast down by the news. But he was adamant about one thing. He flatly refused to write a line unless it was irrefutably demonstrated that Hillary was dead. 'You don't know what that man's powers of resistance are like—but I do,' he told reporters.

When it was all over, with Hillary recovered and the expedition completed, John was able to joke about the incident. 'I had such confidence in Ed's resilience,' he told me afterwards, 'that my heart just wouldn't have been in the writing of that obituary.' But even as he spoke I could see how thinly the satire covered the real distress John Hunt had experienced.

We were finished in the Himalayas about the end of June, and in November I was back in London, meeting Bunny Fuchs at the time when he was able to present me with his first detailed blueprint for the Antarctic crossing.

A whole year of Fuchs's lobbying and backstage pressure was beginning to pay dividends. In January 1955 the big chance

48

came with the opening of the Commonwealth Prime Ministers' conference in London. Churchill was bowing out, Eden bowing in.

Bunny received a phone call asking him to attend in person at the conference to outline the Antarctic plan for the benefit of the assembled Premiers. He did so, gained their support, and soon the money was slowly rolling in. Churchill had started the ball with a British offer of £100,000.

New Zealand in some quarters was not at first notably responsive, though an initial contribution of £50,000 was soon agreed. The truth was that a vein of insular boredom with the 'useless' wastes of the Antarctic continent ran through many a New Zealand heart, in which warmth was really not felt for anything that was not directly concerned with those basic national industries, butter, meat and wool.

An acute illustration of this attitude was revealed in the story of three New Zealand farming men who were lounging at a hotel bar while they listened to the local mayor put forward a plea for financial support for the Antarctic journey.

'Ed Hillary reckons there's a great future for New Zealand down in the Antarctic,' said the mayor. 'How about a contribution to the funds of the expedition?'

At which point one of the farming men took a long pull at his beer, slapped the glass down on the bar, wiped his lips and said: 'The Antarctic? How many sheep to the acre does it carry?'

By July 1955 our organization in London was beginning to hum. We had our executive offices a few hundred yards from the Houses of Parliament, and it was fascinating to be caught up in all the planning.

I met my colleagues. Just names at first. David Stratton, who was deputy leader. David Pratt, engineer. The glaciologist Hal Lister. RAF Squadron Leader John Lewis, in charge of flying.

I think we were the first explorers in the history of British

49

Polar expeditions to be paid a monthly salary. It was not a bulky pay packet for Antarctic pioneers—£500 a year for bachelors, £700 for married men. Still, it was something, and most of us would probably have gone for less, or even nothing.

It was Bunny's idea that I should go as expedition photographer. Personally I was prepared to join the expedition as a mountaineer, a New Zealander, a general handyman. But soon I realized that everyone had some type of specialist skill, and I was glad to have photography for mine.

Organizing food supplies, fuel, vehicles, chartering the ship —the Canadian sealer *Theron*—that would take us on the first long voyage to the Antarctic, where we would land the advance party of six men . . . these and a thousand other jobs kept everybody busy in London till November. And on the fourteenth, one year to the day since I met Bunny Fuchs and heard his plan, *Theron* sailed. There was biting cold in every Londoner's bones that day. I drove down to the Millwall Docks, carried my kitbags past the policeman, through a maze of crates to where the small white ship was tied up—at the end of a long boulevard of beer bottles.

CHAPTER VI

The Bird and the Beasts

EVERYTHING was small in *Theron,* and there was hardly room to move. I caught my head on every doorway, was forced to turn sideways to climb the steep stairs, the poop deck was cluttered with winches, lifeboats and water pipes, and the well-deck was invisible, buried deep in cargo—our Antarctic cargo. This included an aircraft in a box, a second aeroplane with the wings stowed but otherwise ready for flight, thousands of gallons of petrol and paraffin, cases of oil and greases. There was also a Sno-Cat sealed up in a protective cocoon.

On top of all, in wooden crates, were the dogs—twenty huskies bought from Eskimos in Greenland and four pups supplied by the Whipsnade Zoo.

I found my allotted cabin, dumped my kitbag on the floor beside one of the two bunks, then blinked hard and felt apprehensive when I saw a small bookshelf jammed with eleven volumes of Proust. They belonged with the kitbag marked 'Derek Williams'. My cabin companion was an oil industry film photographer who was accompanying us on this first voyage.

Between England and the Antarctic lay ten thousand miles of water. I was not enamoured of the long crossing, for although new countries and new continents always attracted me I hated the process of reaching them by ship—I was always sea-sick.

51

After motoring quietly down the Thames the heavily-laden *Theron* lay at Gravesend for a few hours waiting for some last-minute items. From there we butted into the Channel, and until we passed the Canaries a week or so later, I and several others spent most of our time suffering the miseries of sea-sickness. After calling at the Cape Verde Islands we sailed down the Atlantic towards Montevideo on the coast of Uruguay. Sailing lazily after the sickness, our days were broken only by eating and drinking and feeding the dogs.

By this time I had lost any fears about Derek Williams that might have been sparked off by the sight of all those Proustian memoirs. Derek was a highly entertaining cabin-mate, a dedicated photographer always looking for something of 'deep' significance. 'Make every frame a Rembrandt' . . . no lesser ideal was his attitude to film making.

On the wall of our cramped cabin quarters was pinned a map of the Antarctic continent which helped considerably to while away the hours when I lay miserably in my bunk. I was attracted by the simplicity of the blank white wastes and especially of the bold red line drawn slap through the South Pole bull's-eye in the centre; a geographer's dartboard.

The 2,000-mile journey across the continent via the Pole was planned to last a hundred days—Bunny Fuchs's nice round figure which was to become a startlingly accurate estimate. To accomplish this, the expedition would be away for three years. First we would take *Theron* to the Weddell Sea, establish a base and land the advance party of eight men. At the end of the first year, on the far south side of Antarctica, a New Zealand support party led by Hillary would search out a route towards the Pole, along which we would complete the crossing.

Our aim was by no means original. Forty-five years ago, just as the First World War broke out, another Trans-Antarctic Expedition under Sir Ernest Shackleton sailed from England with the same purpose: to cross from the Weddell Sea to the Ross Sea, using dog teams. Their effort failed, and their ship

Endurance—a frail wooden vessel of 350 tons—was caught by drifting pack ice, gripped and squeezed, drifted for seven months, then crushed, and was sunk. Shackleton and his men took two lifeboats and stores right on to the ice, manhauled them to where there was open water, and saved themselves. It is a dramatic story, one that never palls in the re-reading. One member of Shackleton's expedition was to exercise a certain influence on the leader of our exploration party in the nineteen-fifties. Sir James Wordie, Master of St. John's College, Cambridge, was chief scientist with Shackleton in the *Endurance*, and it was he who first encouraged Bunny Fuchs in the days when Bunny was one of his undergraduates.

Our voyage slipped by in uneventful hours. Apart from feeding the dogs and cleaning their kennels there were no duties. We read and talked and slept; there was no room to play deck games. Lazy days down the sea-lanes. I recovered from the sickness but Hannes la Grange, the South African meteorologist, never did, though he continued taking his turn in feeding the dogs and cleaning the kennels, and with the more nauseous tasks was quietly sick again.

The captain, Harold Marø, we all liked, and he turned out to be a strong determined sailor. Although only thirty-nine he seemed older, his hair was grey, his face lined and off-white in colour. He had suffered several years' starvation and ill-treatment as a prisoner of war in Singapore. Harold had the clear blue eyes with the faraway look; the abrupt statement which served as conversation; the wry sense of humour; the pre-occupation with his ship—all the qualities of the story-book sailor.

I was slow in getting to know the crew. The three deck officers, Canadian by adoption, were Norwegians who spoke Norwegian in conversation with one another. But *Theron* was an easy, friendly ship. The deck crew of six were all under twenty-one and all were on their first long voyage. Some of the engine-room staff I hardly ever saw. As we sailed along the coast of South America, I caught rare glimpses of pallid, etiolated greasers who blinked silently in the sun.

Approaching Montevideo the warmth decreased, the sea turned more green, less placid.

And here was committed the first of three 'crimes'. Nobody had the slightest desire to offend against the folklore of the oceans, but it happened; and though sailors are nowadays less troubled by the old superstitions, deep-rooted traditional fears still die hard.

It started with the albatross, the first I had ever seen.

We were all hanging over the taffrail watching a young, beautiful bird soar effortlessly over our wake in search of food. With delicate plumage, and with rather less black marking than the more mature bird, its mastery of flying was wonderful to watch. The albatross soars, with its long pinions outstretched (its wing span is often as much as twelve feet), swooping effortlessly along the trough of the wave without a flap of the wings.

At sunset we were in the middle of our meal when Roy Homard, the engineer of the advance party, burst into the cabin.

Roy was roaring angrily: 'He's shot the albatross . . . the silly bugger shot the albatross . . .!'

Two or three of the party rushed on deck, others sat and questioned Roy who was still noticeably upset.

It appeared that one of the engine-room greasers coming on deck at the end of his watch saw the lovely bird, went below and returned with a semi-automatic pump-action shotgun. Roy, who was on deck when he returned, was enjoying the evening, and could not believe his eyes when, as the bird swept all unsuspecting over the stern, the greaser aimed and fired. The albatross crumpled, falling badly wounded into the water.

Why, why should the fool have done such a thing? We never knew—it could only be put down to utter lack of imagination in a man who cared nothing for the bird's beauty, nor its freedom, nor its innocent right to fly the seas, nor for the fable

54

(which he probably would not know) of the Ancient Mariner. He was merely a bored sailor suddenly eyeing the object of a moment's sport.

The young albatross, bloodied and doomed, was left flapping around in the green sea, and *Theron*, now cursed, sailed on.

We came slowly into Montevideo in brilliant sunshine. The sea was now blue and the skyline of the city was sharp . . . it reminded me of a film set, a façade with not much behind it.

Here Sir Edmund Hillary and his deputy Bob Miller joined the ship, having flown by the tortuous air route from New Zealand (which lies just across the ocean as the crow flies) over the Pacific north to Hawaii and north to Vancouver, then south along the American continent to Mexico City, Lima, La Paz, Buenos Aires and Montevideo.

It was good to see Ed Hillary again, to renew the link of expeditions. We had been together on the same adventures for five years, and I was glad when our bantering companionship returned immediately. I was also interested to see what would happen to Ed's restless, turbulent energy when hemmed in by the size of *Theron*. During our mountain journeys his mainspring for action was always 'a battle against boredom', or so he said. I think now there was a good deal of truth in his jest. Marriage had made him—if not fat then at least well padded, certainly a figure of contrast with the lean angular man of five Himalayan journeys. There was another minor change: instead of waxing enthusiastic over a beautiful blade of ice surrounded by unknown valleys, he now produced snapshots of his wife Louise and their baby son. This much was certain, though: the heavier Hillary had not grown softer.

Bob Miller was to be Ed's deputy with the Ross Sea party and I was meeting him for the first time: a man of high principles, practical and tough, earnest, absolutely direct, a brilliant geodetic surveyor with a robust sense of humour. For him the Antarctic journey was a boyhood dream come true. Ed had the greatest respect for his first lieutenant.

55

The short break at Montevideo soothed our anger at the shooting of the albatross, and forgetting the incident *Theron* hooted blatantly down the Rio del Plata, passed the sunken wreck of the German battleship *Graf Spee*, then rolled across the cold Antarctic currents to South Georgia. In five days we moved out of the tropical oceans into the frigid waters around the southern continent. In five more hours we slipped across the Antarctic convergence of currents where the sea temperature drops, the air is freezing on the ears, and the sea birds appear in thousands. South Georgia, our last port of call before entering the Weddell Sea, came into view in the evening light after an azure day.

A solitary mountainous island with an ice-plastered backbone uplifted high, South Georgia lies on the fringe of the Antarctic at a point where the latitude is the same as England's. There the resemblance ends. Glaciers sweep down from the peaks and poke their tongues into the sea. There are no trees growing on South Georgia, only a tough golden snowgrass and some emerald green mosses that sprout in the cold bogs.

At first the island appeared as a mountain range floating on an immense blue swell. Even the pink summits which glowed in the sun seemed to be heaving in tune with the advancing ridges of water.

Next day at dawn, after a little more than four and a half weeks at sea, we approached the mainland where a narrow fjord invited us in. Between the mountain walls we slipped, while Cape pigeons, snow petrels and screaming gulls swept around the ship. Green seas burst over the headland as we sailed into calm water. Now the island stood still for me. A small whale-catcher hurried past, dragging three dead whales floating and lolling like bloated slugs.

Theron smartly rounded the point, and with a flick on the rudder and a back kick on the propeller, Harold Marø berthed her neatly at King Edward Point.

Surrounded by tussock, a hardy alpine-like grass, the few

houses of the island sprawl on a spit of land; there is a post office, a generating shed, a meteorological office, and, standing apart and beyond, a stark white cross looking out to the white peaks with its arms akimbo. The cross, somehow disdainful of the settlement, is a memorial to Shackleton, who died there of heart failure during the voyage of *The Quest*. His grave, one among a little collection of whaling men, their resting-places formally fenced with white stakes, is marked by two wreaths of flowers made of tarnished copper and a rough-carved granite block . . . *Ernest Shackleton, Explorer*.

At Grytviken we put the dogs ashore and allowed them to run and roll in the snow. In one way or another we had had quite a time with the dogs. Housed singly or in amicable pairs in their thick wooden crates on top of the piles of deck cargo, they nearly all had their own adventures and sea-going idiosyncrasies. At one stage Tio, one of our three bitches, was with pups. As we crossed the Equator she was showing signs of giving birth to her pendulous litter.

Ralph Lenton, a gifted handyman of the advance party, made an enclosed pen around her kennel and watch was kept. From the bridge the crew would often call down to Tio and she adored being the centre of attention. She sat on her haunches with tongue lolling out, a look of excitement in her eyes whenever anyone passing stopped to talk. As day followed day Tio grew bigger and was petted more and more.

The expected litter day was anti-climax, however, for no pups were delivered. David Stratton decided that Tio was so pleased with the attention that she was delaying the births on purpose, so she was shifted forward out of sight behind the Sno-Cat which lay beside the foremast.

Occasionally dogs got out of their crates and ran loose. This was usually discovered by the noise of a fight or by the remainder setting up such a cry of envy that we heard the din and quickly investigated. One day a bitch called Kuse broke free by gnawing through the two-inch by one-inch packing-case. No alarm came from the other dogs. She could not be traced, and it was feared she had gone overboard.

Another search was made, and we found her flattened miserably and fearfully under some cases stacked on petrol drums. She was nervous and wild. David Stratton soothed her, gave her a drink, put her in a kennel and boarded over the hole. Within a few hours she had cut through and gone again. A fresh search found her again in hiding, her mouth bleeding from where she had torn at the boards of her kennel. A few hours later, without having shown any sign of pregnancy, she gave birth to a litter of five pups.

Shortly after this Tio followed suit—in jealousy, it almost seemed, with an air of realization that her popularity had been eclipsed.

As the pups grew we named them after members of the crew. Marø was the most promising, big and powerful, and he grew to take his place in the teams that reached the Pole—the only pup to do so. Of the remainder Willy, a fat, cheerful dog, and Alf, a shy, insecure, but brave dog, became the much-loved companions to the advance party until they developed an odd paralysis and died. Jonas, who was rather simple but engaging, went as a pup to Halley Bay and died of paralysis and madness. Of Squibs and Mary, the two bitches, Squibs was an intelligent emotional creature who was later put down, there being no place in a team for her.

At Grytviken the Auster was also brought out of her cage and dressed in her wings so that the pilots, so long earthbound, could taxi into the bay on floats to join the sea birds in lively flight.

Several tons of whale meat were purchased for the dogs. Freshly delivered to the jetty from the whale factory across the bay, it lay in great steaming chunks of quivering red meat flecked with tendons. All hands manhauled it on to the foredeck where it was pierced and hung with twine from the railings round the bow.

For sheer carnal spectacle there was nothing I had ever known to compare with a whale factory. It was the super-colossal butcher's shop in the Cecil B. de Mille tradition. Plastic-covered men, with knives like hockey sticks, run their blades into the hugest of nature's creatures. Winches and wire ropes peel each new carcass like a banana. The skin slithers across an acre of blood and grease and is gobbled up in big masticators. New men with new knives dismember the bleeding body. Limbs, tail, flippers and big side fins crash like tree trunks as the winches pull. Then the meat goes into steaming vats and the bones are consigned into the most frightening crushers which smash and grind with a demonic fury.

Within an hour the seventy-ton leviathan is gone. Another takes its place, and the spectacular ritual begins again, a continuous performance in full colour of the carving of a dozen Moby Dicks a day. The smell is objectionable, pervading everything like some new variety of polluted, insipid air. But about the men who go whaling, the silent bearded company who all seem to be people of exceptionally strong character, there is nothing insipid.

Sharp contrast is everywhere on South Georgia. The mountains dominate, standing mostly with their heads in the clouds. The ocean surrounds, majestically isolating the whole island. At the head of a fjord on a shelf of shingly moraine, the debris of a shrunken glacier, stands the whaling factory of Husvik, devouring and rumbling and smoking like a satisfied resident dragon.

Blood stains the sea around the factory mouth, which emits the familiar smell and the familiar noises. But there is also a feeling of orderliness and contentment. Our party were invited to dine with the manager. In the evening light we strolled along the beach where little waves lapped on the fine shingle and the odd beachcombing penguin could be seen pottering.

The manager's Norwegian house was some distance from the factory—set apart across a stream and reached by crossing a bleached wooden bridge. I expected something different from a factory, but nothing as civilized as two white-coated servants to take our coats, sumptuous carpets, central heating and tall exotic plants by the windows. In every room hung colourful and exciting oil paintings—some of them his own, some Gauguin-like nudes, and a few unmistakably *avant-garde* creations. A glistening cocktail bar with easy chairs and occasional tables were placed with thoughtful carelessness.

After the drinks we dined at ease and in elegance, and I listened fascinated by the talk of whales and whaling. At a certain time the manager checked his watch; excusing himself, he moved to a tape recorder which he switched on. Music from hidden speakers filled the room. This music was being broadcast to the catchers out at sea who used the wave-length for local weather forecasts and as a homing link. (They collected their music from radio programmes and symphony concerts when they were at home in Norway.)

By the time we walked back to the ship, glowing with good wine and filled with admiration for an empire controlled from such civilized headquarters, the moon was shining over the fjord. The ship's companion-way seemed much steeper and definitely inconsiderate, the cabins rather austere, the bunks altogether too functional. In this state we reflected on the morrow: and the morrow meant reaching the Antarctic Circle. For me it was a place of geographical magic; in fact, there was only one other geographical point that excited me more—the Pole itself. The Pole has a full name, a simplicity and personality like Everest. Tomorrow we would sail south into the Weddell Sea, across the magic circle—sixty-six degrees south—to the silent seventies.

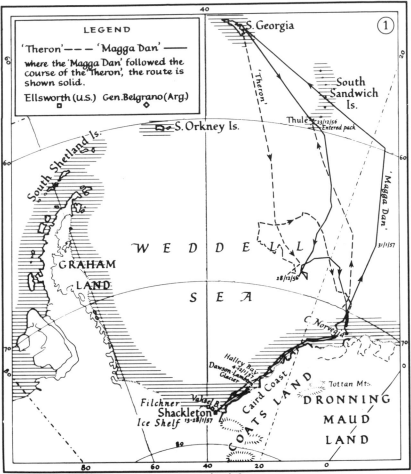

Royal Geographical Society

CHAPTER VII

At Sixties and Seventies

I HAD no preconceived idea of what pack ice would be like, only the usual vague picture of a frozen white lumpy sea. And what we encountered was not at all what I expected. Sailing in the Antarctic pack was in some ways like sailing on the Norfolk Broads. Much of it was like the River Ant, with twisted winding lanes that led through flat acres and acres of fields, except that these were fields of white ice.

Every dozen miles or so we reached a Barton Broad or a tranquil mere whose waters were rippled by the wind with floating ice lumps instead of thick green reeds.

The main excitements came when we found the ice blocking our vital leads, the navigable pathways which were our only route through the pack. And here was the chief contrast between Antarctica and the gentle Norfolk waterways. For where the Broads sailor must turn about and find an alternative channel, *Theron* was obliged to charge, like a bull at the cape.

Just before each impact the engine was stopped. For a moment all was quiet, and you could watch the bow wave creaming away to a ripple. All vibration ceased while the ship glided in towards the silent ice. As the bow crunched into the soft edge the noise was no louder than a sigh. But then, *thump!* and another thump, and another. The entire ship was convulsed, shuddering, riding and writhing up in nautical epilepsy as it smashed the ice into huge floating islands. The cracked lumps—lumps the size of a saloon car—grumbled along the side of the ship as the motor throbbed once more, urging us into the next little reach of winding waterway. Harold Marø's eyes would be cast ahead and around, not always searching for the immediate twists and turns, but for certain dark shadowy marks on the underside of the clouds—which reflect light or dark according to whether there is water or ice below. With this 'water sky', as it is called, no great compass accuracy is possible and our direction was only approximate as we went through the maze, trying to work our way south-east.

Ever since leaving South Georgia there had been an air of greater anticipation as we moved rapidly south, waiting for the ice battle to commence. Much more intently and impressively was Harold Marø itching for the fray. He grew in size throughout these days, became more tense, and more spasmodically jocular as he released the tension. His two chief officers, Karl and Jonas, walked about impatiently, soon to be joined by Sven, the chief engineer, who found it difficult to remain below.

A few days before Christmas—midsummer day in these regions—we were rolling and pitching in a blue-black sea, many of us sick or subdued. Waves spilled over the bow, spray lashed constantly over the deck cargo. The dogs cringed and shivered.

Bunny, who was never sea-sick, watched and waited or sat poring over his charts of all the previous voyages into the Weddell Sea. Ed lay on his bunk above Bunny, whistling tunelessly and reading Westerns. I pottered about doing a bit of filming and processing of stuff that I had shot in South Georgia. I had made myself a corner in the wash-room where I could do a little printing.

At sixty-three degrees south, shapeless chunks of ice were strewn in the sea. Without our noticing that such a change had happened, the rolling eased. The sky was grey, without contrast or colour. The sea was flat and sullen. Across the water *Theron* seemed to increase her pace. The wake swept aside the bergy bits of ice—bits that stuck out of the water two or three feet and were anything up to thirty feet wide. Some pieces hit the bow with a resounding clang.

Harold climbed to the crow's-nest and slid into the chest-high barrel. The engine-room telegraph and steering control were then switched to his lofty control point.

I stood on deck and looked up at him. The steel mast seemed to be alive, I imagined it bent forward—straining to see ahead, as the captain did. In concentrated isolation Harold was in control.

By the evening of December 22, without our realizing the moment of transition, the battle had commenced.

At first the pack ice was thin and open. With an occasional judder *Theron* forced forward. The tension for us was gone, everyone relaxed, talk was livelier and we all stood on the bridge-wings or hung over the bow to watch the thin pack ice split. For two days we sped through, making 160 miles each day. So far, the battle was going easily, as the ice log showed:

22 Dec. 1955　Midday position 62°S, 32°W.
G.M.T.
17.00　Scattered growlers [small pieces of ice].
19.45　Open pack ice.
21.30　Open pack.
22.15　Scattered growlers, pack on either beam.

23 Dec. 1955
01.35　Open pack—Ringed penguins on floes. Visibility 2 miles.
04.30　Open water.
05.10　Open pack—leads running E–W—6 snow petrels; 2 silver-grey petrels.
07.40　Pack ice opening out—1 Adélie penguin.

64

08.00	Open water—1 leopard seal.
09.00	Three large tabular bergs 3/6/9 miles.
09.30	Very open pack. Many leads—bloody tired.
11.30	Entering close pack 9/10th cover.
11.55	First Emperor penguin.
13.20	Crossing large pools—3 Emperor penguins.
16.00	Close pack. Visibility 1 mile. Larger floes.
17.00	Stopped in close pack—visibility ½ mile.
17.35	Proceeding close pack—visibility 1 mile.
18.05	7 Antarctic petrels, 2 crabeaters.
19.05	Close pack 8/10th cover, larger floes.
19.50	Stopped in close pack—snowing, poor visibility.
20.40	Under way—poor visibility. 2 Antarctic petrels.
21.10	Crossed Antarctic circle.
21.50	Coasting down W. side of large pool. Visibility 2 miles.
22.10	Close pack 8/10th cover, medium floes.
22.45	Stopped in close pack, poor visibility, snow and drift.

On Christmas Eve, although we were making progress south, there was a change in the sea and ice around us. The ice cover was becoming thicker and heavier, and soon a high wind began pressing the ice together.

24th Dec. 1955

01.10	Still stopped—poor visibility. 3 Antarctic petrels.
04.00	V. slow progress 9/10th closer, harder, thicker pack.
04.55	Close pack—large deep floes. Visibility ½ mile.
05.55	Entered pool heading 104° 1 mile [?] wide, visibility ½ mile. 2 Emperors, 8 Antarctic petrels, 4 snow petrels.
06.50	Leads tending S.E.
07.05	Close pack 9/10th cover, ship stopped.

07.55 Started engines in close pack.
10.50 Stopped engines—no progress.
14.20 Small leads, close pack 8/10th cover.
14.40 Close pack. Visibility improving. 3 leopard seals.
15.40 More leads—ice thicker (ten feet).
17.00 Stopped engines in small pool, close pack—no visibility.

Harold came down from long hours in the crow's-nest, sighed gloomily and said: 'It's no good, I can't see. Let's all have a drink.'

While Karl stayed on watch we began our celebration of Christmas by eating dinner on Christmas Eve—a Scandinavian custom. We all ate in a small cosy mess-room where the tables were waited on by Gunnar, the chief steward, who was the only teetotaller on board. Christmas dinner, Norwegian in time, was Canadian in character: chicken soup, turkey and cranberry sauce, with strawberries (carried frozen) and ice-cream. Food aboard *Theron* was always good, with unending supplies of fruit juices, steaks, chickens and turkey every Sunday: I have never eaten better food at sea.

The singing of songs was in progress when Bunny slipped out for a walk on deck. He returned to say that we had been cut off by a large floe astern—pressure was forming along the side. Harold bit his lip and left us.

About two o'clock on Christmas morning the pressure eased, and in two hours of backing and charging Harold smashed free. Then through Christmas morning we made better progress; there was still no sun but our hopes had bounced high again.

It certainly did not seem like Christmas. The day was light for twenty-four hours, and although this was a novelty it was Christmas in a flat, unchanging and sterile land compared with the fogs, frosts, flashes of winter sunshine and the celebrations of England.

66

Around the ship in twos and threes were grey-white and black-headed Antarctic petrels, the virginal white snow petrel, and occasional Emperor and Adélie penguins. Under the cloud it was a strange, silent, relentless, colourless world for them— and us.

We were not going south easily. After twelve hours of southing we were suddenly forced to double back on our tracks to find a way out of an unbreakable part of the maze. At 67° South on Christmas Day our track on the chart looked something like the wanderings of a seasonal reveller, as can be seen from the map on page 61.

As I went in to lunch we were almost stationary, grinding against a huge unmoving bank of ice, trying unsuccessfully to push through. In the crow's-nest I could see Harold Marø searching for an alternative. Suddenly we made it. The ice broke with a crash and he jammed the prow like a wedge into the break, and kept it there, pressing open the ice for a new lead.

After a lunch of roast turkey, Christmas pudding and a beaker of Uruguayan wine, I stood again in the bow. The ice cover was less and we steamed into a great Broad. At three o'clock Bunny called up to the captain: 'Will you stop the ship and let all listen to the Queen's broadcast?' He waved assent. The telegraph rang—the engines died and stopped. The anthem boomed out and the Queen's voice came through in strong and firm tones. She alluded to life being like a voyage of discovery and mentioned the explorers of new lands. We all took this to mean us personally. A dozen of us were crushed into the radio room—Bunny, Ed, John Lewis, Ralph Lenton, John Claydon, and Hannes with a pipe clamped firmly in his jaw, and a couple of the crew. Everyone seemed to be projecting himself away to his home—I know I did.

Later in the afternoon we killed a seal for dog meat, dragging it redly across the ice. Hauling the carcass inboard, however, the hook and tie slipped, and the seal gurgled and sank, leaving only a few blood-red bubbles on the ice to record its end. It did seem a pity to kill, especially as this effort was all wasted. As a rule the unsuspecting seals had no fear of us when we walked up to them, even with rifles in our hands. I never got used to this necessary slaughter.

On Christmas night the ship stuck when trying to break through ice that was nine or ten feet thick. For three hours we could not shift. Ahead the ice was thick and hummocked. After trying repeatedly we broke loose and moved back to another place. But still we could not get through.

During the night the ice thickened, the noise of the ship smashing and grinding was continuous; but in the early hours we broke out and made some seven miles along narrow leads. The clouds drifted away and the sun came through revealing the first really clear skies since South Georgia. In the sunlight the ice was transformed into gleaming green and white. The water was blue. I spent happy hours on a rope and wooden jib filming over the ship's bow as it smashed its way through.

On Boxing Day the ice became thicker than ever and was rafted into rows—it looked like raked hay. Four tabular bergs could be seen ahead.

In the afternoon we battered through towards a pool in the ice. It seemed large enough to fly from, and on deck Bunny decided to send the Auster on an ice reconnaissance. It was not easy, however, to reach the clear pool, and we were stuck fast for three hours. All was ready for flying, yet we could not smash through to the open water. The engines were stopped, and while a conference in the chart room was going on, someone said: 'The icebergs are moving towards us and the floes are breaking.'

The mate whipped out of the chart room and ran up the steel rope ladder to the masthead. The engine turned, and as the ice split along the side of the ship we backed into a tiny pool, turned, and headed away towards the large pool. By

9 p.m. the low fog cloud had lifted and the sun was brilliant.

In the pool we stopped. A lifeboat went over one side and the Auster over the other. Even though sunny the evening was bitterly cold, with frazil ice forming on the sea like fat solidifying on the surface of a stew cooling in a saucepan. With the lifeboat we cleared chunks of drifting ice from the pool and John Lewis thundered off, in the dramatic knight-errant take-off that he loved to make. Then he flew on a thirty-mile arc around the ship.

By eleven John was back with news of good leads and better water to the south-east. We set off. The ice had turned pink with long blue shadows reaching from the hummocks. The water had an oily texture, opal green in colour.

At 11.30 p.m. the sun was still shining and the ship was moving forward in wonderful ice scenery. I was fascinated by the sunshine at midnight and stayed up all night to stare over the miles of ice-covered sea. Frazil ice was forming in the clear water patches—before my eyes a skin of clear ice took shape. In other patches where the thin ice was broken and the sea spurted through, it was frozen in delicate shapes with petals which are called ice flowers. The low sun lit all this new world in a pastel light of theatrical beauty.

But in the first narrow lead we jammed. The ice held on for five hours while the propeller turned, frustrated. The rudder flicked and the ship's bow growled and twisted, attempting over and over again to come loose. Eventually we broke through but made only a quarter of a mile in the next seven hours. Ahead lay measureless acres of white misty pack with hardly any water showing. We jammed again and waited, hoping the wind would move the mass enough to allow us to move on.

Early next morning, strong winds from the north-east began to close the floes yet more tightly around the ship. The ice pressed and twisted, buckling the sides of the ship. Below decks as we lay silent and helpless I could hear the twisting and scraping of the steel ribs as they braced against the pressure.

And so could everybody else. The captain paced about and swore; the crew stood about smoking. The noon position showed that we had moved twenty miles.

The ice all around us was drifting south-west: we did not easily believe it, but the fact was that *Theron* was impotent. Despondency reigned for the day, and everybody lay about given over to frustration. Everybody, that is, except Roy Homard—who went over the side with a saw to experiment with building an igloo. Having built it he then had the courage to sleep in it.

By the afternoon of the 27th there was no change . . . we stopped fighting in the heavy pack, waiting for visibility and the ice conditions to improve, for a strong wind was now causing the whole of the pack ice to move faster and press more tightly together. *Theron* braced herself against the strain—it seemed as if she had her sides puffed up and was holding her breath.

For the next four days we made no effective progress. At first we waited in listless inactivity; it was not easy to talk, for there was nothing much to talk about: it didn't seem right to joke or laugh. We soon grew tired of the inactive hours stretched out on a bunk. So we would sit for hours over coffee. Some philosophized about life in tedious discussions, some played cards. Contract bridge caught on like an epidemic. Not quite everybody was affected—perhaps half, and with a third of us the disease lasted throughout the voyage.

It is difficult to create a cogent word picture to conjure up the idea of our crazy progress through the pack. Imagine first the great ice-field around you. The atmosphere on board is full of tension; you feel you want to push on but you are encompassed by this mass—as far as the horizon—of floating, drifting, moving pack ice. It comes in large floes, sometimes as big as a tennis court, or a football field; and sometimes ten miles across . . . huge floes, packed together, with narrow lanes

70

of water leading through them—lanes which become smaller whenever the wind or tide begins to press them together.

Like a mountain glacier, this is a live mass, and its life runs in slow-motion. Without warning, the pack ice begins closing, and equally without warning it can open up. We could either stand on deck to watch the drama, or hang over the prow which was more exciting, or climb up the mast and sit on a small crosstree just below the crow's-nest where the captain was.

Going into the ice is no single act; it doesn't strike like a blow, nor sweep up like love at first sight—the slow-motion act is its most striking feature.

As you approach, the demeanour of the sea changes—it begins to smooth down, grows quieter, and there may not be ice in sight at all.

Men were all the time going up to the crow's-nest on the masthead, and always the radar was watching. Throughout the ship the feeling was the same . . . 'It's coming—it's coming —the ice is coming slowly.' But hours go by before you move into parts where there are bergy bits, drifting in the water, and then you get long icy strands—and then it all drifts away again and you steam ahead for ten more miles with no ice in view.

When we first hit the ice proper, continually banging and hacking our way into the stuff, the ship had enough impetus, enough power and weight, to go on thrusting. But when we reached the ice-fields and were completely surrounded, except for the little leads running in between, the technique was changed. No longer was *Theron* powerful enough to thrust and shove and elbow her way forward. The ship stopped dead. We had smashed a lot of ice which now lay as rubble alongside. Before it began to solidify and become packed around the ship like cement, the captain would have to put *Theron* into reverse, turn the propellers and gradually pull us out.

Later, when he began to chop his way into solid floes, the

71

bow went into the ice like a sharp axe into a tree. Difficult as it is to pull an axe out after a blow, it was even more difficult to extricate a ship, and Harold Marø had to use all the skill he possessed. Then he would strike once more, never in exactly the same place . . . then into reverse and out again. In this way he hacked through . . . five or six feet at each chop, and sometimes he had to chop through three hundred yards, carving an alley for *Theron*.

One morning we tried hosing sea water, pumped up from warmer depths, along the ship's side. In a tentative fashion we also experimented with digging—but the pressure held firm.

We took the dogs on leads for long runs over the ice.

We played more contract bridge.

Despair was intensified by the news that *Tottan*, the supply ship of the International Geophysical Year which had left London a week after us, was now ahead of us. She reported that she was at latitude 70°S and making ten knots in completely open water. *Tottan* had had the advantage of our radio information, and now she was two hundred miles away to our east. This was bitter news for the captain and Bunny, confined in a ship that could hardly budge.

Two days later the floes began to move and the pressure on the ship eased a little. We then began a determined effort to release her.

With axes, crowbars, picks and shovels we dug around the bows and sides, removing tons of ice. At the bow Gordon Haslop and Tony Stewart drilled holes in the ice and lowered charges. These were detonated, but at the end of sixteen hours' digging and dynamiting nothing happened.

We went to bed.

Next day we chopped away several tons of salt-free ice and loaded this inboard to use as fresh water. In the afternoon we dug more ice away from the ship.

Then unaccountably whole acres of ice began to move. To me it was imperceptible, but the captain suddenly cocked his

Digging away
ice from *Theron*
in the
Weddell Sea

Theron stopped by pack ice

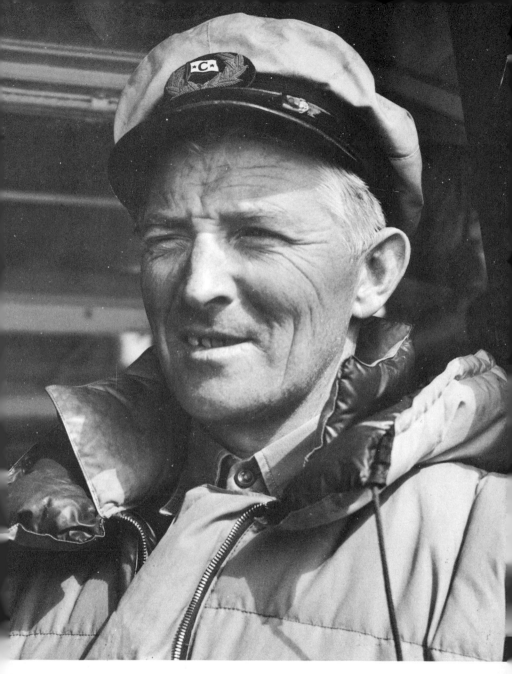

Harold Marø

Whitenose

Top left: Ken Blaiklock   *Top right:* Roy Homard

Below: Shackleton, a collection of black dots—men, stores and dogs—on the Filchner Ice Shelf as seen from the air when we returned on 12th January 1957

Hannes la Grange

Hal Lister

Roy Homard and David Pratt fishing through a hole in the ice during a winter snowstorm

head on one side, balanced on his toes, watched over the side, and then without a word sprinted for the mast to start the engines.

Just as the loudspeaker in the wireless room announced to the world on the six o'clock news that *Theron* was stuck in the ice, making no progress, we slid out—to float freely in soggy water. Everybody cheered and ran around the ship looking wild-eyed and happy. Harold Marø once more hurled the ship at the ice, smashing through half a mile. . . .

And then we stuck again.

All night we were over the side digging beside the ship, with poles and axes pushing and levering the huge frozen chunks away from the sides. A mad nocturnal punting party, poling away under the midnight sun. All we lacked was the pretty girl with a parasol—and a punt.

By removing broken ice from the stern and working along the ship's side, the ship would be able to wag her tail. By cunning use of the rudder and power, the captain could then winkle his way out. . . .

The size of these hunks of ice varied, but generally with crowbars and poles it was possible for ten men to prise them loose; then they were pushed astern and the propeller chopped them up so that they could float away. For dragging the largest pieces we used a ship's winch.

Days went by and we dug and dynamited, making sometimes nothing and sometimes a mile. With the wind and current we drifted a long way north and west until we were nearly back across the Antarctic Circle.

The ice of the Weddell Sea was like a slow-moving whirlpool —at least that was our theory; later I began to feel we did not get far enough away from the ice that was being affected by the whirlpool action. It was as if we were on the outer rim of a huge catherine wheel; the leads that ran into the ice ran to the centre, and sailing thus into the heart of the pack, we travelled considerably further west than we bargained for.

73

Friday the thirteenth was Black Friday indeed—and with a new moon.

We were trying to ram ourselves between two gigantic floes, each of about fifty square miles with a few inviting feet of water lying between.

Each of these ice floes, the largest I had ever seen, was some five miles wide. From the masthead the skeiny threads of water could be seen to join, but from deck level the ice presented one unbroken flawless surface, as if we were trying to sail across a solid white table; and Harold Marø was now attempting to work *Theron* through the middle.

On this day I climbed the mast to sit and watch from my favourite position, the crosstree just below the crow's-nest, often occupied by Bunny or Ed when I was not there.

As usual I had three cameras, one loaded with colour and one with black and white, these two around my neck and the movie camera hanging from my wrist on a strap. Weighing nine pounds, the movie camera was an awful handful on these occasions, for the ship lurched and quivered every time we charged the ice, and I always seemed to be climbing the wire ladder at a crucial moment.

Harold was at the helm in the crow's-nest, tense and intent. In the bitter wind of the grey day his head stuck out of the barrel and, knowing I was just below him, he would toss out cryptic curses on the ice projections and lumps as he tackled them. But mostly he was silent, grinning pugnaciously.

Theron should have been amphibian, I told him.

I soon gave up trying to poke my camera at him when he was working like this, for he was self-conscious about my efforts to photograph and shied away; so I decided not to break his concentration.

Seventy feet above the steel deck I clung to a stanchion with my legs, kept one arm around a projection on the mast, and waited for whales to surface, or to film any spectacular phase of the ice-breaking. The mast whipped frighteningly, and steel

74

cables slapped and whined while the ship juddered forward.

As *Theron* curved around between the two gigantic floes, the lead suddenly narrowed. A huge projection—a cape of ice, in fact—made the gap absurdly small. I wondered vaguely about the width of the ship, which seemed much too broad to get away with it, but Harold was already sizing up the chances of slipping *Theron* between these fangs of the ice floes, and he increased the ship's speed.

'Wonderful,' I thought, 'he's going through.'

We charged the gap at full speed, Harold hurling the ship under full power. I felt we were a fat thread approaching the resistant eye of a needle.

Harold did not take it straight for the centre but aimed off to starboard, and as the bow came within a few feet of impact I began filming.

With a tremendous crash we made contact, *Theron* rising several feet, twisting out of the water like a porpoise before diving for the gap, taking with her great scrapings of paint-stained ice.

The bow bounced off the one huge floe and into the gap. Harold was playing billiards with her, making a cannon off one floe across to the other, hitting hard to gouge away the ice and if possible set the big ice cape in motion.

Now we were hitting the port-side floe. Nipping off another big scraping, *Theron* straightened beautifully and slid further along the gap.

By this time I was clinging terrified as the mast whipped violently and tried to fling me away. Embracing the steel pole I pressed the cameras into my chest for protection. All the same I could not help being fascinated by Harold's fantastic game of skill. It was incredible to watch how he judged the power and weight of the ship as he smashed into the floes, playing ball with nearly a thousand tons. He was worried all the time about *Theron*'s safety, and we as landlubbers knew well enough that he was half destroying his vessel to get us through.

75

Below me I could see blue-grey water churning. *Theron* slid through almost full length, but with a sickening lurch came to a stop, gripped half-way along the hull by the two monster floes. Harold kept the engine-room telegraph at 'full ahead' and looking from his eyrie swore at the ice below.

Theron thrashed the water but the jaws held fast; we all knew the danger of this bite, which gripped the ship's vulnerable underbelly at two points; we were caught under pressure in a giant rat trap.

Harold shut off the engines and climbed down the mast. I let go my grip and followed him.

Already Ed Hillary and David Stratton were going over the side with axes and crowbars to cut away the ice. Nearly everybody went eagerly into the attack, my own enthusiasm being so great that I put my cameras on one side and completely forgot to use them.

We worked all night, for sixteen hours hacking and dynamiting at the ice jaws, but gave up as the wind and tide pressed the two floes more firmly together. The ice piled up as the pressure increased, until we had ice standing *above* the height of the well-deck.

The heavy side plates of *Theron* began to buckle. Fortunately the ship did not burst, though she certainly was bent. We chipped and chiselled with crowbars to no effect. John Lewis suggested another round of bridge and we played with our attention on the wind, watching one another's expressions as the ship gave tiny moves and sighs when the pressure grew stronger.

Luckily, after a few more hours, the pressure eased off and the lead gently opened. At last we could sail north in comparatively easy ice; although the floes were still nasty, the way was open—and without the awful rat trap pressure.

Altogether *Theron* was stuck about a hundred times; twenty of these predicaments were really serious, and this the most serious of all.

76

Three weeks in the ice had now gone by and still there was an exhilaration to be found in hanging over the bow or sitting on the crosstree, watching the ship rip and ride through the enormous banks of ice.

Sleeping was difficult, especially for those whose bunks were in the bow. David Pratt and Bob Miller had bunks just above water-level, where the noise was awe-inspiring. Only three-quarters of an inch of steel plate stood between their bunks and the ice. They gave up sleeping there because of the terror it caused, quite apart from the noise.

For a time we all went into the cabin to experience the thrill of standing within inches of the impact. The throb of the engines caused the bow to vibrate in a steady shake, but as the forward power was stopped before hitting the ice, the bow became suddenly still and silent. Outside could be heard the rustle of water. The moments would drag and always too soon we expected the impact.

'Take a quick breath.'

'Brace your legs, brother.' And then. . .

Up lurched the bow, up and up, with a rending tearing sound that stopped our hearts.

Nearly always we turned and ran.

CHAPTER VIII

The Emperor's World

ANY hope that the ice battle might decline once we were free of the big floes was soon tempered by a new and aggravating phase of this snail's-pace advance.

For a whole week we worked right around the clock in the effort to make headway, but *Theron* achieved in the first three days only half a mile. Embedded in the pack ice around us were fourteen icebergs.

Before long the prow was beached on the ice and she rested like a stranded whale. All paint had long been stripped from the hull; we were now leaving a brown scar of rust on all the ice we touched. The ice generally varied between ten and thirty feet deep; so deep the ship was riding her bows on it and yet not breaking it.

As the days went by we developed a formidable technique for attacking these ice problems. No orders or directions were issued; there were no rosters of working hours. Whenever the ship stopped, groups of men went over the side (with a single step down from the well-deck we could stand on the ice) armed with axes, picks, poles, boat-hooks, ropes and dynamite. The ship's wire ropes were slung over forward and aft, and by using the anchor winches we could drag great islands of ice. The winching wire was used just like a cheese-cutter; we were able to sever chunks of ice by wrapping the three-inch cable round it, standing back, and giving a tremendous pull until the wire sliced through. Then we could pole the pieces along the side of the ship, pushing them to the rear, and when we had enough at the stern everyone would stand clear while Harold Marø churned up the ice with the propeller.

Our most eventful, most menacing days were without doubt the 18th/19th January. We were jammed head-on into thick ice with a huge floe on either side holding us immobile. Gordon Haslop used a small charge of dynamite to crack the floe on the port side, and although only a pound of explosive it was close to the underbelly of the hull just near the engine-room.

The tilting floe that held us cracked. The ship lurched (those inside swore it lifted a foot out of the water), and in the engine room panic reigned. The chief engineer ran white-faced on deck shouting Norwegian oaths. The warning to the engine-room that we were dynamiting had been forgotten.

We never again set off charges along the side of the ship, not only because it shattered the nerves of those below but also because it tended to buckle the hull. Charges fired at the bow, on the other hand, struck the ship in her strongest part and were carefully used as shock, to give the propeller just that extra urge it needed to break the ship's inertia.

It was a day of incidents. Nine pounds of dynamite were used to crack off an ice island, but the charge was unwittingly placed in soft ice that was rotted by seeping water. This sent the blast upwards instead of against the ice.

Ice flew into the air and rained down like flak. I ducked under a ventilator. Although frightened I couldn't help feeling amused by the antics of the others diving for cover.

Fortunately no one was hit—but several holes were torn in the wings of the Auster.

The second incident almost cost Ed Hillary his life. A group of us were on the ice cutting a path, and the ship's winches and wire ropes were being used to remove our rubble. Suddenly, while the wire rope was being returned to the deck winch, the rope fell into the water.

The ship's engines were going full ahead. Ed Hillary, Bob Millar and I were perched on floating ice pulling frantically on a rope guide line to keep the four hundred feet of steel cable clear of the propeller. A chunky lump of ice, about half a ton, had fouled the cable and pressed it into the stern.

We screamed a warning to the bridge, but the rope touched the propeller as the engine died. The spinning blade caught the two-inch cable and whipped the rope through our hands. Standing as we were on a slippery block of ice, we let go. Ed gave a roar of fright when the rope-end flicked and locked around his ankle.

Bob and I managed to knock it free just before it came tight. A moment later and Hillary would have been sucked under.

The rope-end snaked into the water as the steel cable wrapped itself around the propeller. Ed's face was ashen; and so, doubtless, were ours.

A stunned silence came over everybody. Was the propeller smashed? Would this cripple the ship? Were we to be left without further fight? All eyes turned to the captain. Harold's face was grey and drawn as he hung over the stern. A lifeboat was lowered while he and the chief engineer peered into the water. The propeller was twelve feet below the surface; it was obviously impossible to extricate the rope. Several turns of the steel cable had been forced round the main propeller shaft and actually lay inside the collar of metal between ship and propeller.

In the end we were lucky. After many attempts to free the rope the ship's engines were started. Grating and banging noises were heard but the propeller worked on. In a few days the grinding and thrashing ceased as the steel rope was just worn away.

At another point, backing into deep ice, *Theron*'s rudder was twisted, allowing only the smallest movement to port. This made us a lame duck in a very unfriendly sea, for with a faulty rudder we could not make sharp turns.

The bent rudder greatly annoyed Harold, continually upsetting his judgment as he glanced and weaved through the pack. Next day at breakfast he recounted to us with a wry smile how he had straightened it.

During the night with few people about he grew more and more angry with his inability to turn left. He decided on a desperate device his father had once used in an emergency— and got away with it. He forced the rudder straight by backing into the ice. It must have been a fascinating night of experiment judging by the story we heard.

'I put the rudder hard to port and could only get six degrees,' said Harold. 'Then I rang for reverse and set the ship in motion. Then I rang for "stop engines" and waited while the ship crunched into the ice. After a bit I rang ahead and tried the rudder—it was still only six degrees. So I reversed once again— but still I got six degrees.

'Finally I rang for "full astern" and held the power until I couldn't hold it any longer. Frankly, I was horrified at what I was doing. She rammed into the ice and simply shuddered from end to end. I rang full ahead again and the helm went hard over.

'It worked—the bloody thing worked, I'd hit so hard that I bent it slightly to starboard—and it stayed that way.'

What was even more interesting, the rudder stayed 'that way' throughout the voyage.

Harold was also worried about some of my filming positions which I suppose were sometimes more rash than reasonable. About this time I was anxious to get good pictures of *Theron* charging the ice, and the only method of succeeding was to stand as close as I dared while the ship made her charge— straight at the camera. Thinking about it afterwards it seemed stupidly dangerous, but it is a fact that when you concentrate on the viewfinder of a camera, your eye devoted solely to the problem of framing your picture, the potential dangers of the spot you are in seem somehow to disappear. So I positioned myself on the ice about ten or twelve feet from the edge, looking straight at *Theron*'s bow as she came charging forward.

Harold had thought I would be moving away the moment the ship crunched into the edge, but unless I stood my ground and went on filming it was obvious that the effect I wanted— the full impact of the vessel hitting the ice—would be lost. Well, I got the impact all right, but the ship reared in front of me and shook my little ice plateau so fiercely that from the view-point of the cutting-room much of the blurred result was useless.

During this period, shortage of sleep and the problems of the ice caused a queer season of dreams aboard *Theron*. John Lewis recounted how one of his began with the ship forcing her way slowly through the ice-covered sea. Then suddenly *Theron* began to steam *uphill*.

We all hung over the bow, said John, to watch the progress. Up and up we steamed, over a crest—and then without any difficulty sailed across green fields with black and white cows and windmills turning and people waving as we passed by. For a few seconds of the Antarctic night John was back for a day in England.

At seven o'clock one evening we had a long-delayed burial service. At the request of the family of Joseph Miller, late bos'n of *Discovery II*, his ashes were to be buried in Antarctic waters in accordance with his last wish. With a short simple service read by Bunny the casket was slid over the side in sight of the icebergs surrounding us.

This was the second of the three incidents which had an undoubtedly disturbing effect on the crew. Firstly the shooting of the albatross—and now it was learned we were carrying the ashes of a dead man aboard, another infringement of super-stitious sea lore. We of the expedition party were aware of the intention to perform the burial at sea, but to the crew it came as a rude shock, and there was a definite stir of feeling at the time of the ceremony, though no one uttered a word of protest regarding the last rites for Joseph Miller.

In fact, the manifestation of this feeling of disturbance was (I think subconsciously) reserved for an altogether different object. For several days we had been flying a white nylon wind-sock, using it as an air-marker and wind direction-finder for the aircraft sorties. Being pure white, however, and with a background of white ice, it was difficult for the pilots to see the thing clearly. Someone then had the bright, if macabre, idea of dyeing the white wind-sock red . . . by dipping it in seal's blood. This was done, and the red nylon flown on the mast.

It was during, or just after, the burial service that Karl, one of the officers, raised the subject of the seal's blood. He did not think it right, he said—and there was an indefinable air of approval among the rest of the crew as he spoke—that blood should fly at the ship's masthead, and he firmly requested that the wind-sock should be at once removed. Karl made no mention of the burial, nor of the albatross, but it was clear that these things were also in his mind. At all events we took down the offending red symbol.

The harvesting of fresh water from the sea was a strange ritual to be performed each day. Normally we kept fresh water in the forward tanks, but one of these tanks was now fouled by sea water infiltrating through a ten-inch split in *Theron*'s bow, and the water in other tanks was discovered to be frozen solid. From that moment the taking of baths, even a morning wash, had to cease.

Each day we cut our supplies of fresh ice direct from the sea. During the process of ice formation all the saltiness conveniently drops out. We kept the stuff stacked on the deck and melted it down in an old oil drum.

As the days drifted we became more accustomed, though never reconciled, to our strange, silent surroundings. Excursions

83

into the ice grew more regular, and more distant, as we absorbed the fact that *Theron* was virtually a part of the fixed landscape. At first we just walked over the ice to photograph the ship, to chase penguins or collect seals. In places the sea could be seen through the cracks, sometimes in pools.

On all these walks I found my senses became keyed to the highest sensitivity. The ice moved, it was alive, it grunted, it sighed, with the pressures from afar pulsing through and seeming to give the ice itself a pulse.

Seals swam and made curious metallic clinking sounds as they searched for breathing holes. But the most frightening noises were made by the whales when their nostrils appeared in the minutest of pools. Blue-black skin could be seen glistening and the big nostrils opened. Air and condensation steamed out with the startling suddenness of a train in a station. Within a few seconds the whales were gone. When the high, hard and dreaded dorsal fin of the killer whale periscoped into the pools I felt as naked and just about as brave as a visitor inside the lion's cage at a circus. I always stood stock still, for I had read somewhere that these jackals of the deep were known to smash the ice from underneath if they thought seals or penguins were lying above. It may be an old wives' tale, but I did not know for certain and was disinclined to risk sacrificing myself in the cause of finding out.

David Stratton made the longest journeys. On skis he went several miles to climb the icebergs and search for signs of pools or open water. John Claydon, who was later to become the pilot for Hillary's party, went off with tins of yellow dye, searching for ice floes flat enough to use as a take-off strip for the Auster. Despite many determined surveys, the ice was too hummocked and rough for even the most quixotic attempts, although both Claydon and John Lewis were by this time ready to try anything.

Our excursions were a nature ramble with a difference, always with the ship in the ice as the centre point of our orbit.

And always the penguins could be depended on to provide the best hours of fun we had known since the voyage began.

Chasing the lively Adélie penguins was irresistible. It was almost impossible to catch one, and judging by the joyful manner in which they ducked, dived and evaded, never actually running away from us, it was easy to believe that they positively understood the game.

When, eventually, my film sequences were shown, I was disappointed that every penguin shot had been deleted. Arguing from the reasonable principle that the prime object of the film was to depict the crossing of Antarctica, the backroom powers went on to insist: '*Every* Antarctic picture is full of penguins—this one will do without them.' The result: not a fleeting sign of a penguin anywhere near the Antarctic continent. It was a pity, especially as our chasing games had made entertaining material.

In one area of rough ice David Pratt and the geologist Jon Stephenson were chasing an Adélie penguin with a verve and concentration that was pure Chaplin, and I was able to shoot a good footage of film showing these antics. The two men and the penguin were slithering and leaping around the boulders, sliding on their stomachs, diving down pinnacles of ice—a fine pantomime which ended with David unexpectedly catching the bird and settling down to stroke its head and flippers. An altogether delectable little scene that was ruthlessly dropped from the film. Why? 'Because there are no shots to show that you eventually let the penguin go free—and that might offend the animal-lovers. . . .'

The Adélies were the young, gambolling children of the ice, full of excitement and wonder—in marked contrast to the elegant, solemn Emperor penguin with his waddling, thoughtful gait.

Earlier in the New Year we had seen our first Emperor, very tall and thin, all alone in the wilderness, standing motionless in the middle of a huge ice-floe. It seemed inconceivable that anything could live there. For three days he did not move, and apart from an occasional wriggle and twist in our pressure bed, nor did we.

It was just after Sunday lunch that I caught sight of our lonely sentry moving for the first time. He spread his flippers, raised himself on tiptoe and pointing his beak into the sky, stretched and yawned so excruciatingly that I twitched in sympathy. Then, shrinking again to his hunched shape, he resumed the dejected posture.

No doubt the solitary bird knew where he could get food. And did he drink? I never saw a penguin drink.

The peculiar adaptations of the penguin never ceased to astonish me. What powers of resilience to withstand the monotony of perpetual silence! What a vacuous mind, or was it placid serenity? The Emperor was said to be the most intelligent of the penguins; some say that the early embryo of the Emperor is very primitive and that he is of ancient origin. To be so intimately, stubbornly adapted to so inhospitable a climate and so barren a land is undoubtedly some proof that the penguin has been there for a long time.

The Emperors exist during the summer months, sometimes in twos and threes but for the most part singly, fishing in the sea, resting and meditating on the ice-floes. As the sun sets for the winter they migrate south to their nesting grounds, there to gather in flocks numbering thousands. Sleek and fat and shining in their black, white and gold, each member of the bowing, waddling community then begins to search for a mate. In the sunshine their feathers sparkle like sequin suits on television idols.

Only an Emperor knows who is another Emperor, and, yet more important, who an Empress. No external differences of sex can be detected, a ludicrous complication of nature which always seemed to me unnecessarily unjust in the already hazardous milieu of their lives.

Having chosen their loving companions they settle on a

square foot of old ice where, in time, each Empress lays an enormous off-white egg. It is dark and cold in the middle of winter, with the stars winking and wheeling in the black sky.

The nuptials and honeymoon ended, the Empress now dusts her flippers, steps away from her creation—and leaves the adoring Emperor to hold the baby.

Jean Prevost, a young French ornithologist, made an interesting study of the rites. Among other theories he believed that 'childbirth' for the Empress was often agonizingly painful, possibly causing death. According to his observations, just before laying the egg, which is incubated by the male partner for between sixty-two and sixty-four days, the two penguins separate from the rest of the rookery, which establishes itself from March each year on the ice.

They stand together for several hours stamping down the snow in the same spot waiting for the 'birth' to start. Then the female begins to shake with contractions so violent that she sways and sometimes shuts her eyes. After a few minutes the egg begins to appear.

Prevost describes how, after the egg is laid, the two birds perform a kind of dance and sing to each other before carrying out the exchange of the egg, which the male frequently strokes with his beak. Their different songs, he found, are the only way of recognizing male from female without performing a dissection.

Within three hours, however, all this marital interest has disappeared and the egg has been given to the male to be incubated between the tops of his webbed feet and his paunch. The female meanwhile has left the ice for the open seas to feed for the first time in two months.

The Emperor proves to be the most domesticated and long-suffering of deserted husbands. Manœuvring the egg on top of his feet, he raises his toes and stands on his heels. With a flap of warm skin and feathers under his belly he then slumps over the egg for six weeks. Endless time ticks by. As the sun returns, spreading light and hope, the egg is hatched. Faithful Father, now almost atrophied in every joint and attenuated in every limb, stretches himself before hobbling to the sea to bring the baby's food. Temperatures are probably sixty degrees below zero but he finds a way, down through fissures, into the water, and gobbles the krill which lurk in the warmer depths. The female has long since departed—or so observers relate. Perhaps the observers decide their gender by dividing them into lean and fat. At all events the male bird feeds and protects the young, who grows rapidly from fluffy chicken with markings like a panda, into a large chubby bird covered with a somewhat moth-eaten plumage.

Six months after hatching, the young birds are left to fend for themselves. They swim away into the Weddell Sea, presumably to find their own isolated ice-floe on which to pass their days in severe meditation.

When we went close to our solitary wanderer, the floes were shifted by *Theron*'s passing. The Emperor stood with his back towards us, head bowed as if in grief. We shouted rudely across to him and for a moment I thought he would turn. Here was his chance, his only chance perhaps, of seeing a ship and her crew from the lands of warmth. But when I looked back he was still standing upright, motionless and disdainful, ignoring our presence and looking to the empty horizon.

Around midnight on the 19th the second mate, Jonas, broke the ship free from another of the familiar ice traps and made a mile to the west towards some pools of water that could be seen forming.

By the afternoon of the following day we reached a pool which from the masthead seemed a great lake to our eyes; but Bunny and John Lewis were looking anxiously about for something a little larger. The sky was grey, the sun weak and low on the horizon. Harold nosed *Theron* all round the pool, still aching to smash along the frailest lead. John Claydon, whose turn it was to fly a sortie, was not in any doubt—there was a chance to fly and he was going to take it. He wriggled into his rubber-sealed immersion suit, and with Gordon Haslop and Ken Blaiklock began plotting his flight in the chart room. Bunny gave his assent. Before long everybody was galvanized into action.

Ed Hillary went aft with the crew to lower a lifeboat and I went with him to clear small ice chunks from the pool. Peter Weston had repaired the Auster's damaged wings—his sewing was immaculate; he was now preparing the Auster with a silent, rather fretful care.

The pool was irregular in shape and along the longest run a crosswind of a few knots was blowing. This run was about three hundred and fifty yards in length—and John Lewis was saying the Auster would need between three hundred and fifty and four hundred yards as a minimum. I had a word with John Claydon before he stepped over the side, telling him I wanted to film the take-off. 'I'll do two runs,' he said, 'the first just to get the feeling of the pool. The second will be the take-off. I'll have to curve the run to try and get some advantage from the wind.'

The ice lumps were cleared, *Theron* nosing into the downwind end of the pool to give Claydon every possible foot of water. He fired the cartridge starter and the little motor bellowed defiantly. He taxied about, warming the motor, and turned tightly at the end of the pool within five yards of the ship.

We saw him ram open the throttle and he crouched forward in his cockpit ready for the run. The plane leapt ahead, planing on the floats. Then he started the exciting move—a curving take-off. Rapidly gaining speed he curved his run to take advantage of the length of the pool and the wind.

The Auster bucked and heeled over as he careered along, holding her on the very point of capsizing. Half-way along the pool I fully expected him to throttle back—but no, he thrashed on, straightened his run, and just when it seemed to us that he was certain to smash into the ice at the end of the pool, his floats left the water. This was no dummy run; he was airborne, still with his nose down just over the ice to gain better flying speed.

John Lewis turned and spoke in his most matter-of-fact manner. 'Damn good—I knew it was long enough,' he said.

John Claydon gained height, set course over the ship, and for the next three and a half hours everyone listened to his voice coming over the loudspeaker. He kept a flat commentary going as he went north, but excitement crept into his voice as he saw open sea and the ice thinning-out to nothing. I had loaded a camera for him so that he could photograph the leads.

Before John returned everybody was impatient to be off. According to his reports, if *Theron* fought only a few more miles of heavy ice she could get leads that would take her to the open sea sixty miles to the north.

As Claydon circled to return to the ship, John Lewis, acting as flight controller, gleefully sent him a warning. *Navigational warning—there are whales on your landing strip* . . . to which came the reply: *That's quite all right—I've chased wild pigs off the runway before now.*

It was true that two whales had come up to breathe, and porpoise slowly about in the water, but the Auster settled in as beautifully as any sea bird. I asked John why he cancelled the trial run he had talked about. 'I decided to take off there and then,' he said. 'I just hadn't the nerve to do the thing twice.'

A report was given and *Theron* churned into the ice around the pool. At last there was a definite line to follow out of the morass that had held us for a month. *Theron* charged, twisted and shuddered as of old; she became a live thing again under Harold's hand.

'I'm going to land you boys on Antarctica if I have to break the ship's ribs,' he said.

Two miles from the pool we were caught by a huge floe. We tried dynamiting, but the pressure began to pile ice around the ship faster than we could move it. For forty-eight hours we fought and almost cried with frustration. So near and yet so far.

Higher than it had ever done before, the ice piled up along *Theron*'s sides. The ship groaned under the weight. Despondency struck again.

By now the frigate H.M.S. *Protector* was sailing into the Weddell Sea with the aim of telling us where the ice edge lay. She did not intend to enter the pack herself in case she too was caught. But *Protector* had two helicopters which could be of great use in finding leads through the ice.

About midday on the 22nd the floe that held us split, and the pressure eased off. *Theron* backed out and for twelve more hours made slow progress to the north. Nobody wanted to go to bed, so we sat up all night watching as the ice opened out.

Seventy miles to the north *Protector* waited in open water, and when her helicopters made contact on their third attempt *Theron* was making half-speed through the ice with all of us waving from the rigging.

Late in the afternoon we sailed into open water and rose gently to the swell. The ship was certainly battered, and her captain chastened. All on board were relieved to be free.

The meeting with *Protector* was an oddly memorable rendez-vous. Now we were north of the Antarctic Circle again, the sun was setting for the first time. We parted after dining on board and thanking them for their help; as a gift several crates of beer were stored in the longboat which rowed us back to our ship. *Theron* hooted and steamed away ready to continue the fight. Heavily outpointed in the first rounds, she was still somewhat groggy, but more than ever determined to win.

We headed north-east, occasionally cutting our speed to half while passing through leaden grey seas flecked with ice and icebergs. Then we turned south again across the Antarctic Circle. The sun was a shimmering orange orb as *Theron* steamed through the pack ice that was turned pink by the evening rays. The sea, rising and falling in a long swell, was also pink.

Another lone penguin rode on the magic carpet of ice, standing with his back to us and disdaining, like our first Emperor, to take even one look at the only ship he would probably ever see.

We sighted Antarctica on the 26th of January.

Snow showers swept the ship as we picked our way carefully through dozens of icebergs drifting along the coast. Beyond lay the continent.

The first view was not particularly memorable—only un-broken cliffs of ice, like the icebergs except that these were longer, swept by driving sleet and snow.

Theron now went southwards at full speed. The moat of cold blue water along the cliffs continued save for occasional patches of drifting sea ice. Behind us we left a perfect line of rippling wake which ran away till it lapped on the nearest ice. Seals lay, a few singly and some in clumps, along the coast. On the body of every seal that I could closely observe there were great scars and many had open wounds, a bloody indication of how frequently these creatures encountered—and escaped from—the killer whales and the carnivorous leopard seals.

Vahsel Bay, our original destination at the head of the Weddell Sea, was now only a few days' sailing away. To port the continent rose in a cliff and swept inland to a high horizon. To starboard the pack-ice edge lay only a league away. Ahead was a great fleet of tabular icebergs. The temperature dropped to 19°F, much colder than we had been having.

We sailed in and around the silent fleet of bergs as the sun came out for the first time in many days.

At 8.40 in the evening, with the sun still high in the sky, the landing flags of the British IGY party were sighted. Two lonely-looking figures stood there waving.

From the clear water of Halley Bay, Bunny and John Lewis flew to see if the way inland beyond the base was a practical proposition for vehicles (if there were no breaks in the sea cliffs further south we might even have been committed to using Halley Bay as a base). The Auster reached the heavily-crevassed

Dawson Lambton Glacier and was then called back by flying control who reported that ground fog would prevent a safe landing.

The ground fog cleared. A few local flights were made and then John Lewis and Ken Blaiklock flew inland to map the glacier. This attempt was foiled by low cloud.

Next day, although the skies were grey, Bunny decided to try another flight and settle the possibility once and for all of using this site as our base. Gordon and Ken once again flew inland but again no clear view presented itself. At two in the afternoon we decided to pull up the anchor and sail south. The ten men of the IGY base were left waving forlornly from the beach.

In the next bay, a mile from Halley Bay, was an Emperor penguin rookery of more than five thousand birds. Several chicks with black and white feathers round the eyes bobbed and paddled in the water like swimming pandas.

Sailing further south met with everybody's approval, for we all wanted to see the base set as far south as possible.

During the night Bunny and the captain were among the few who stayed awake. An immense field of pressured pack ice lay in our path. Fortunately the captain found a break in this— a continuous channel a few chains wide where pressure had split the field in two, so for several hours he sailed along this canal watching the shattered pressure ice on each side, standing sometimes twelve to fifteen feet high. Harold watched apprehensively, for if the wind shifted the jaws would come together. We'd had our fill of that medicine.

At 5 a.m. Ed Hillary woke me to say that a possible landing site could be seen. We stood in and dropped anchor within a stone's-throw of our haven. The water was deep and from it the ice sloped steeply to a terrace. But this *was* a possible unloading site.

The Auster flew again, first with Harold to judge the state of the surrounding pack ice and the safety of the ship if she unloaded at this point, then with David Stratton to look for seals and generally see over the area. The day was perfect, the temperature 12°F, and with the crispness of the weather came crispness of decision and a vigorous desire to get ashore. We were all anxious to land and get cracking.

Bunny wanted to make sure that we began unloading in the right place, and certainly the choice of the correct site was crucial. Vahsel Bay, fifteen miles away to the south, was a bay that was iced over and ran into a steep-sided valley where bare rock showed black between the crevassed ice-covered hills which rose to three thousand feet above the bay. The bay itself was studded with small icebergs and the waterfront was a jumble of ice ridges like row upon row of barbed-wire entanglements. From Vahsel westwards the hills dropped abruptly away, with level but crevassed ice lying like a giant ploughed field several miles wide. Beyond and still further westward the furrows in the ice ran out on to a smooth ice shelf 150 feet above the sea; the shelf stretched inland as far as the eye could see.

Bunny and Gordon Haslop flew off in the Auster, into and around Vahsel Bay, over the ice shelf and its crevassed junction with the hills, probing west along the shelf where it sloped into the sea, then inland some forty miles to stare at a level white nothingness that met the blue horizon.

Aboard *Theron* we waited in the sun. David Pratt's mind was already leaping ahead, working on the problems of how we would have the tractors tackle the slope behind the terrace we could see. Deck crates were being opened and shiny tractors cocooned against the long sea voyage were emerging from their swaddling clothes. Steel wire ropes were cut from the petrol drums on deck. Sledge-hammers demolished the flimsy wooden deck railings that had been built hurriedly in London. Dogs howled and leapt about in the general excitement.

Quite suddenly this landing site was discarded. From the air Bunny had chosen to land on the ice shelf proper and build the base some thirty miles from the crevassed hills and broken ice of Vahsel Bay. So *Theron* motored off to Vahsel Bay while the Auster was still in the air. Once in the bay the Auster returned to the ship and we sailed westward along the ice front. At a point where sea ice formed a convenient landing, *Theron* lay alongside and we jumped ashore. With axes we dug into the ice, then buried some heavy timbers; to these we anchored *Theron* with steel wire ropes.

Days of the week had little meaning. It was a coincidence that we began unloading on Monday morning, 30th January. The skies were again clear, the temperature just above zero Fahrenheit with a biting wind coming from somewhere near the Pole.

The dogs were the first overboard. They rolled in the snow and jumped for joy, quite mad with delight. Next went the Sno-Cat and the Auster, leaving the hatches of No. 1 hold clear. From three in the afternoon we worked hard to get the two Ferguson tractors and two Weasels clear. Hut timber, rope and general cargo had to be manhandled until we could use the tractors.

At midnight we dragged ourselves to bed dog-tired.

On the second day loads of stores were dragged from the ship across the sea ice to a dump at the foot of the 200-foot climb up the sloping ice shelf.

The hut site for Shackleton—as we decided to call our base —was chosen on a level ice shelf two miles from the sea-front.

By evening on the second day the Weasels were relaying loads up the hill to the hut site, while the Ferguson tractors took stores from the ship to the dump at the foot of the hill.

On the third morning we began unloading early. The day was cloudy. After the previous days it felt warm—the temperature was 20°F with a north wind blowing from the sea. One of the Weasels developed track trouble and this caused some difficulty in synchronizing *Theron*'s unloading with the haulage from the dump to the hut site. By midday a great number of boxes and stacks of hut timber were piled on the sea ice beside the ship.

But the tractors roared on in the grey mist. Long icicles and wigs of hoar-frost formed on all the ropes and cables. The wind increased in force. Quite suddenly the sea began to rise, and soon it was bursting in waves over the ice front, swamping the ice in slushy water. *Theron* rose and fell, rubbing her battered side on the ice.

The unloading went on grimly.

I was driving a tractor-load from the ship across the sea ice to the dump when the storm got going in earnest. On the return journey to the ship it became more and more difficult every yard to see the way ahead. The wind, sleet and snow lashed my eyes.

By four o'clock a full gale was blowing.

CHAPTER IX

Toehold at Shackleton

THE storm was a bitter blow. Wading up to our knees in the slush of ice and water, we tried desperately to rescue the stores and equipment that were soon floating everywhere.

Shortly after four o'clock the whole area was awash. Unloading from the ship was halted, and parties were struggling frantically on the ice in an attempt to move cargo away from the heavy swell which swamped the ice front. The steel wire cable holding the ship to the shore kept slackening and tightening, and under the strain the wire sang a curious note—almost a dirge; we kept away from the wire and its unwholesome ditty.

What proved to be the last load was hitched to my tractor and I hurried away inland. In the flying snow I nearly collided with Ed Hillary who, head down, was making his way back to the ship.

At the depot I met David Pratt coming down the hill with the Weasel. I passed on Bunny's order that everyone was now to get back to the ship as fast as possible, then David took my load and was gone in a flash up to the Shackleton hut site; he was to bring back David Stratton, Bob Miller, Ralph Lenton and Peter Jeffries.

I turned my tractor towards the ship. Visibility was now only a few yards, snow and sleet plastered my goggles, eyes and face, and I was able to keep direction only by steering straight into the blizzard with one arm hiding my face from the lash of the wind. Beard and eyes were soon packed with ice particles.

It was impossible to judge how near to the ice edge of the sea I was driving, and I began to get nervous, so I stopped the engine and went forward on foot, feeling my way; then I stumbled back to the tractor to climb aboard and once more grope ahead for a few yards. All the time I was looking ahead in hopes of seeing the shape of the ship looming through the snow.

Forward on foot again, investigating, then running back to the tractor like a motorist caught in a blind fog—but still no sign of ship or sea. Suddenly I saw something black near the wheel, stopped and leapt off. It was a dog curled in the snow and I had nearly run over it. I abandoned the tractor and struck out on foot to where I knew the ship would be. At the ice edge I found the rest of the party still wading among the stores, boxes floating in the ice slush and water sweeping in with each wave.

But *Theron* had gone.

I had not realized that as the storm increased its ferocity the ship had been ripped away from the edge, the cables to the ice anchors snapped. When this happened Harold Marø started his engines and disappeared into the blizzard, shouting through a megaphone to Bunny and three or four others who were left on shore that he would try to get back to them. So I joined Bunny and Ed Hillary, Gordon Haslop, Roy Homard and Ken Blaiklock. For a while we used a small rowing boat to salvage the equipment, but we were all feeling utterly frozen, our feet and clothes were wringing wet, and we gave up the effort.

'Keep together and watch for the ship returning,' Bunny called out.

A minute earlier I had laughed for the first and only time— a shade hysterically, when we were nearly up to our waists in the slush. With the aid of a rope I was hauling packing cases, and there was one big crate bobbing in the water beside me as I heaved and strained. For some reason I was momentarily entertained by the words of a stencilled inscription on the floating crate . . . PROPERTY OF THE BBC—HANDLE WITH CARE.

Then, like a ghost ship through the storm, *Theron* suddenly appeared. She was painted white and to all of us seemed something of an apparition. The captain's voice, yelling urgently and not a bit ghostly, soon jerked us into the realities of our plight. Through the megaphone Harold roared the news that he was about to try coming alongside. . . .

'But I can't tie up . . . you'll have to jump aboard while we're on the move!' shouted Harold.

Somebody in our party gave a rhetorical cry: 'What the hell does he think we're doing—jumping a bus in Oxford Street?'

But within minutes we were all grimly aware that Harold had no choice. The wind was blowing him hard towards the ice, and it was necessary to bring the ship close enough for us to leap at the rope ladders that were being tossed from her side —yet not so close for *Theron* to hit the ice on which we stood; for if that happened the result would be tragic, it being ten to one that the ice would crack and our footholds simply collapse underneath us.

It was a delicate operation for Marø, and delicately, skilfully he performed it. As the ship churned slowly abreast of our group, the entire crew were leaning over the side throwing ropes, ladders, anything they could find, to help us clamber aboard.

Harold's judgment in the raging storm was superb. He brought *Theron*'s bow in towards the ice just close enough for each of us to make our neck-or-nothing leap to safety. As we jumped the ship kept on the move, and although we were swung right out over the ice, and although at least two of the jumpers dangled somewhat uncomfortably until they could be manhauled aboard, it was at least something to be thankful for that there were no casualties.

Once safely aboard we peeled off our drenched clothes and had the enormous luxury of putting on dry outfits (no hot baths were possible for we were still short of water in the tanks). Straightaway the warmth and relief of the ship changed the incidents on the ice from grimness to gaiety, and those of us who had been ashore almost formed a club on the spot.

But the light-heartedness was quickly dispelled by the news from the radio-room. There were still five men in great discomfort, marooned inland at Shackleton base site. Stratton, Lenton, David Pratt, Bob Miller and Jeffries had tried making their way towards the ship but were foiled by the storm; they spent the entire night huddled in their Weasel, cold as only the Antarctic knew how to make it, ruefully considering their future if the ship were unable to return.

Next morning the storm had eased enough for the cold quintet to make their way down to the unloading point. Understandably they were puzzled when they found the ship had gone, leaving only a few bedraggled stores and the whining wet dogs. Nevertheless, they were soon taking a philosophical view of the situation, although the ship had to stand off for another twenty-four hours, kept back by north winds that were blowing loose ice up against the front and jamming it tight for an area of two miles.

Theron eventually came up to the ice and we found the five who had been left making a gallant effort to salvage the still-floating equipment. When we brought them aboard they were all studiously casual about their experience.

'Guess what *we* had for breakfast,' said David Stratton ironically. Said another: 'We weren't exactly unnerved by the night in the Weasel, but some of us were certainly a bit shaken. After all, it's not very pleasant to be suddenly ripped away from a comfortable ship and all your belongings—and dumped on the ice without warning.'

100

Theron re-anchored—again to the ice edge, which had not been broken away though it was hammered and scoured by the sea. Now, however, we had a better anchorage on a smoother front, and the unloading continued non-stop for the next five or six days. We had cold and fairly bad weather but never a storm like the angry greeting of our arrival.

We were never long between one trouble and the next. The new problem was that the whole sea was rapidly freezing over. We were into February, the season was getting on, the sun setting a good deal earlier each day. A variety of headaches with the vehicles meant that we were able to dump our stores on the sea ice only half a mile inland. Unloading was held up several times when vehicle parts were found to be out of order, and on this point Bunny had to make important decisions. The choice lay between halting the unloading in the forward hatch and going into No. 2 hold to dive for parts which lay a long way down, covered with countless boxes and crates of hut timbers. In short, we were caught in the cleft stick of having to dump our stores on the sea ice in order to get at vehicle equipment that would put the vehicles in trim so that they in turn could shift the stuff away to Shackleton hut site. Again we went into the dangerous manœuvre of off-loading stores on to the sea ice.

These were not easy days, unloading an entire cargo without any of the facilities available at a normal dock.

A similar hard decision had to be taken on the most vital issue of all: leaving the advance party of eight men who were to become voluntarily imprisoned on the Antarctic continent during the next year. We dumped their stores at the sea ice depot and now the question was: could we with clear conscience leave these men and sail away? For the first time it began to creep up on many of us that the notion of deserting eight people in such a situation was not altogether a happy one. For the first time a feeling of sentimentality about the eight was sensed

101

by those of us who were about to return to England for the coming year.

We went on with the unloading, and Bunny told the advance party to get their personal gear ready because we might have to leave them at short notice. All the time Harold Marø was now pacing impatiently and watching. He was anxiously observing the state of the ice, spending much time in the crow's-nest peering out with his binoculars.

About noon on the crucial day we stopped for lunch, and all those who were near the ship came for the farewell meal on board.

Afterwards I climbed on to my tractor and with several people aboard was about to make the trip to the hut site two miles inland. We were driving across the ice when somebody yelled at me to stop. A messenger from the ship was racing after us, waving furiously.

The message surprised us all. 'The captain says we must sail within the hour . . . Bunny says you've got to get on board at once.'

As things turned out we were delayed for nearly three hours; earlier that morning Gordon Haslop had flown off with Ken Blaiklock, leader of the advance party, to explore the region beyond the base. They were the first men to see the mountains that lay behind.

And then the radio flashed them the message: THE SHIP MUST SAIL WITHOUT DELAY.

We waited for the Auster's return—the tension was really building up by this time—and when the aircraft landed and was taken aboard, Bunny gathered the eight men of the advance party together to deliver his last little speech before we sailed.

'I know it's a risk,' he told them, 'and I am throwing the weight on your shoulders. If you stay here and build the base, the original scheme can go forward. But if we pull out now, if we all go home, it may jeopardize the whole expedition. We shall have no base, no advance party, nothing—and the scheme will be thrown out by at least a year. It's now up to you to make a go of it.'

Bunny had made his difficult decision with speed and without sentiment. The truly heavy burden was placed, nevertheless, on Blaiklock and his men—and they took it squarely. I believe theirs was one of the greatest, if not *the* greatest, of all the contributions that led to our ultimate success. Ken Blaiklock was soon to be revealed as a man of strong calibre. Above all, he had the two prime qualities—as Fuchs himself has—for an Antarctic leader: the ability to wait and endure, plus the mentality for 'keeping on steadfastly'.

The last good-byes were spoken, the gangplank (just an old packing case) was pulled away, and the eight men stood waving on the ice as *Theron* slowly moved off. There was no doubt we were now two parties, the link between ship and shore decidedly broken.

We all felt, and Bunny knew and felt it too, that when we sailed from Shackleton the lot of the eight was bound to be one of hardship. There was a good deal of troubled murmuring among ourselves, and David Pratt said to me: 'I think we've done a bloody awful thing. I hope they will be all right.'

I hoped so, too, as I leaned over the side and watched the lonely group . . . Ken Blaiklock, leader and surveyor; Ralph Lenton, carpenter, builder, and Ken's deputy; Peter Jeffries, Tony Stewart and Hannes la Grange, the meteorologist; Roy Homard, the engineer; Taffy Williams, the radio operator; Rainer Goldsmith, the doctor.

Our departure was split-second timing with huge fields of new pack ice bearing down. If we had left only a short time later we would certainly have been jammed; the sea was starting to freeze, and already the new sludgy ice like wet cement was packing a thick mess around the vessel.

But *Theron* succeeded in breaking away—and we took home a proud but pretty well wrecked ship. The smashed bow had to be welded at South Georgia before we could continue. We had also broken more than half the steel ribs, dented the plates along the side, and twisted the hull. Certainly we had accomplished what we set out to do: unload on the ice of the Weddell Sea and land our advance party at Shackleton. But now, bringing back the battered empty ship, a great feeling of emptiness came over me when I thought of the eight left behind.

We sailed into London with just a bit of white paint still showing above *Theron*'s waterline. The rest was a rusting, tired hulk.

CHAPTER X

Three Leaders

AFTER climbing, working and travelling, in the Himalayas and Antarctica, under the generalship of three of the most outstanding expedition leaders—John Hunt, Ed Hillary, Vivian Fuchs—it was inevitable that I should soon find myself absorbed in the dangerous but fascinating game of assessing the qualities and psychology of leadership. I had never given much thought, however, to the differences between the three remarkable men until a certain sunny day during *Theron*'s long voyage home.

A favourite pastime among the Norwegian sailors was that age-old trial of strength in which two men sit with right or left hands firmly clasped in the taut battle of strength to determine which of the pair can force his opponent's arm into submission—the old trial of wrists and biceps which is often so much more than merely physical, which tests (or so men seem to think) the force of character, and which symbolizes the domination of man over man, establishing the fact of a superior power for all the world to see.

One brawny young engineer in Harold Marø's crew, Alfred, was the undisputed champion at this game, and we were all intrigued when a contest was arranged between him . . . and Bunny Fuchs, who was then forty-eight, and fit as a fiddle. Bunny had already tried his hand in a 'friendly' match, but the second challenge of the champion was the really significant bout.

They sat down together, gripped hands and set about it, the crew watching all agog, though feeling that Bunny did not have much hope of success against the virile master.

They pressed and strained, and as the seconds ticked by the audience all fell silent. The veins on Bunny's handsome head were beginning to swell, his face reddened, his eyes shut tightly as he fought.

Almost a minute passed, and then the Norwegian began to falter. Before long there were murmurs of applause—for Vivian Fuchs had beaten the champion.

And, superficially, that was that. The game was trivial enough and we went about our business.

Far more interesting was Bunny's demeanour during the next few hours. He was oddly elated, jubilant, less severe than usual, and his eyes seemed to glint with the expression of a man who is compulsively determined, almost dedicated, to demonstrate an absolute, unshaking and unshakeable confidence in himself.

At other times during the voyage, and later on our second journey to Antarctica, the pattern was repeated with interesting variations. Bunny, the oldest among us, would throw himself with silent passion into every form of physical activity, every game and exercise, until he could beat every one of us into the ground. Whether it was deck tennis, quoits or squash, even darts and shove-ha'penny, he would play each man in turn till it was crystal clear that Bunny could whip them all at all types of physical prowess. If it turned out that he was not quite up to the standard of a particular opponent, Bunny would practise the game with a ruthless intensity until that standard was reached and finally surpassed.

When there was a spate of after-breakfast P.T. on the deck, Bunny would always do more skipping, perform more press-ups, more of everything, than anyone else aboard. Even at the most strenuous games the powerful, greying leader of our expedition could match himself against three or four people, one after the other, and when he could vanquish all of them several times running, would cast about him for a new opponent. At fifty he was still incredibly strong, single-minded, full of endurance and determination.

In large measure those attributes belong to Bunny Fuchs, and who would or could deny that for a crossing of the Antarctic continent they were fundamental qualities? Bunny was to become one of the twentieth century's heroes—and yet there was a feeling among some who served under him that here was a man commanding our unstinted respect, admiration, obedience, co-operation, but not our sentiments, not our 'affection'. He did not seem to believe in what we called the human touch, and the so-called endearing human qualities looked as if they might even be anathema to his unsentimental eyes.

He pushed the Antarctic expedition through to its end by the sheer force of his willpower. The leader who placed himself—literally, for two thousand miles—at the front of our caravan, also proved himself right on many occasions when others took an opposite view. He proved beyond doubt, by word and deed, that it was possible to land in the Weddell Sea two years running (on this point his critics were utterly confounded). Certainly there was a danger in planting an advance party (and planting it, as we did, so insecurely) under conditions where we might never have reached them the following year. But the plain fact was that Bunny's plan succeeded, and we did return.

In the teeth of controversy and a host of Antarctic problems he then crossed the continent as he said he would. He planned operations almost single-handed, devised his own methods without asking a soul for advice, and issued his succinct orders whenever his mind was made up. Bunny was phenomenal in the sense that he truly did not seem to *need* advice; he gave many of us the suspicion that if it were possible for a man to cross Antarctica alone, he would be that man—so marked were his endurance, confidence and driving force.

He was also the master strategist who stressed the value of the carefully-laid campaign from which not the slightest departure should be made unless it were crucially unavoidable. Unlike Ed Hillary, who from early days had tackled all his problems by means of the bold frontal assault, and who would instantly scrap a good idea for a better one, Bunny was trained in what could be called the school of inflexible-enterprise-without-emotion. Like many a good military commander in the field he was emotionally disinterested even in his most exciting targets, and by the time each goal was accomplished he was already looking beyond it to the next, wasting no effort on savouring the delight of achievement. But then, Bunny appeared not to savour anything, not even food—and certainly not music, which he barred from our base throughout the Antarctic except at week-ends.

Reflecting on these and many another aspect of the main-springs that make explorers what they are, I became aware of a strange quirk in the public portrait of the two leaders, Hunt and Fuchs. Sir John Hunt of Everest was universally regarded (and so many people had told me this) as the stiff, unbending military commander, a just man but formal and unemotional, the efficient army colonel or brigadier. As for Bunny, he was popularly seen in the role of affable pipe-smoking scientist who was on matey terms with all his party, and who in England had the gay and easy human touch.

The truth was that the personalities of both men were switched to something startlingly different when they went into action as leaders in the field of operations.

Bunny Fuchs was like the profile of the continent itself—tough, flat, unchanging, dogged; and after three years in his company I could not say I knew him.

John Hunt was the idealist, who could on occasions be brim-ful of temperamental feeling and sentiment. Far from being the clipped, orthodox soldier, he won the warmth of your heart as few commanding officers could hope to do, captivating and inspiring his party with his own dreams.

At least one among Hunt's ideals might have been, but was never, called trite. After the success of Everest he publicly pushed the well-worn platitude that it was 'team work' and 'team effort' on the mountain which had made the Everest dream come true.

This was not only a fact: it was the essential basis for reaching the summit.

And yet, endlessly put forward to the world by a lesser spirit, the simple fact could have sounded not merely trite but tawdry. Not for an instant was it seen thus, for John Hunt had made Everest into a message, a goal for all human beings. Every man and woman could have their own little Everest, and it was undoubtedly Hunt who fostered the ideal. True, the nature of our expedition was on his side in this matter, the climb to a dramatic summit having been achieved by group effort at a most dramatic moment in time, the coronation of England's young Queen. All the same, Hunt's ideal, born out of the physical fact that two men reached the top of a mountain, could easily have faded away without the dedicated and conscious line of thought which he pressed from the day Everest was conquered.

It is doubtful whether Bunny would find it possible to stomach the notion that Mr. and Mrs. Everyman might find a personal 'ideal' in the Antarctic crossing.

As expeditions go, Everest was unusually emotional, though never more so than on the day that I was lying opposite John Hunt in a tent at Camp III on the mountain, at about 20,000 feet.

We were discussing the organization of the return to England when the expedition ended, as we hoped, successfully, and John was telling me about his family, his wife and four daughters. Although I had not so far visited Britain, had not even met all the English climbers until the start of the expedition, I had a slight bond with England in the shape of an unspoken admiration for a certain piece of work performed by Hunt's wife and children. Mrs. Hunt and her daughters had devoted themselves to a simple chore which made life on the mountain more convenient. They sewed name-tapes on every item of clothing and equipment allotted to each man in the party. I had been rather touched by this, and before the expedition got under way had written a letter of thanks to Mrs. Hunt.

In the tent I recalled the family's gesture, telling John how much I had appreciated their awareness of the well-known 'little things that count'—and in passing mentioned my letter to his wife. At this news John Hunt looked up, oddly surprised.

'You wrote thanking my wife?' he said, his voice hesitant on each word.

'Yes, of course,' I said. 'I naturally wanted to thank them.'

'But . . . that was . . . extremely thoughtful of you, George. . . .'

As he spoke, John Hunt broke into tears. He cried simply, unashamedly, freely, and told me that my trivial note of gratitude to his family had somehow deeply moved him.

A few minutes later he was on his feet, outlining in crisp tones to a group of climbers the technical hazards of the next part of the mountain programme that lay ahead of us. Hunt was an interesting, more affectionate and infinitely more complex character than I had ever supposed.

Four years afterwards, at a vital stage of the Antarctic crossing, I could not help thinking of those tears on Everest. It was when we reached South Ice, after a month's toil and trouble, a month and three hundred miles of arduous travel across the most difficult and dangerous stretch of all.

Throughout this period there had been more comradeship than at any other time, and South Ice was a goal that provoked in most of us a feeling of excitement. After the crevasses, the hazards and hold-ups, there it lay glistening on the horizon. It was just a small oasis on which four of us, many months earlier, had erected a prefabricated shack after being flown in to prepare the ground. It wasn't really a 'place' at all, but to those who built its hut it was like home, and we all got a kick from the sight as we approached.

While we prepared to drive across the silent white expanse to South Ice, Bunny gave a characteristic cold douche to high-spirited emotions.

'Well, there it is,' he said calmly. 'We're going in now. And don't forget—*no looting*!'

The sophisticated flatness of the remark was what made me wonder how Hunt would react under similar circumstances. Bunny and John, I realized now if never before, were poles apart.

John was like the mountains; he went up to high peaks and down the other side—the fighter pilot, the sprinter. Bunny was like the Antarctic; he crossed, dogged and unsmiling—the bomber pilot, the marathon runner.

Hillary was different again, of course. The ebullient, restless Hillary, who hates the 'walking part' of a mountain expedition, who made such gigantic strides after Everest, retained basically the same spirit of adventure and (there is no other word for it) 'fun'. Ed Hillary had always the same attack whether the location was a glacier or a gondola.

It was fascinating to observe also some of the practical points of difference between Ed and Bunny: differences that emerged more and more clearly during the discussions they had while we returned to England after *Theron*'s outward voyage.

In the light of the experience gained that year, Ed was all for making modifications in various matters concerning vehicles and equipment. In particular, he was inclined to reject the type of hut we were to occupy. For our side of Antarctica we had a semi-prefabricated structure that went together like a jigsaw puzzle; it was a wooden framework with large numbers of cross pieces, all carefully numbered, and with hundreds of bolts to hold them in place. Ed's opinion, which turned out to

III

be correct, was that building our hut would be a long and complicated task.

For the party on *his* side of Antarctica he wanted something altogether different: no less durable but more practical and much more simple to erect. So, before he returned to New Zealand to prepare for the Ross Sea end of the expedition, he cancelled his original hut and ordered a new version, a structure prefabricated in big sections, with entire walls that could be rapidly put together. Bunny seemed a shade displeased by this departure from the blueprint, but Ed went ahead with his own ideas and we on our side stuck to the original pattern.

Similarly with vehicles and clothing, Ed was always prepared to scrap what looked like offering the smallest disadvantage. He discarded some of his party's stock of clothing in favour of garments, such as quilted-down jackets, which he thought would be warmer and more protective. Bunny remained content with the clothing issue which had been decided, army-fashion and without attention to individual measurements, well in advance of our departure—and if something ripped, well, you could always find a piece of patching material to carry out the repairs.

On the continent, Hillary's vehicles were at times used right around the clock; as he drove towards the South Pole he worked on a shift system with each man taking his turn at the head of the column while others followed and rested. With Bunny there was no rotation in the management of such affairs. Bunny was the leader in fact as well as title, and he drove at the front from start to finish. When he tired, we halted. When he was refreshed, we moved on. It was a Napoleonic type of command.

On mountain journeys with Hunt or Hillary there was always an element, naïve but enjoyable, of the boyish pirate game. Crossing Antarctica under Bunny's leadership it was as if we were controlled by the disciplined direction of a fine headmaster.

We did not sit around as a party discussing the pros and cons of a move. Pros and cons were announced by Bunny, who worked them out *in camera*. For a man who shared so little of the thinking that lay behind the problems facing us, he nevertheless achieved in us an extraordinary degree of contentment with our lot as expedition members. And whatever reservations we might have had about details of procedure and technique, one thing was certain: our Commonwealth Trans-Antarctic Expedition—Bunny's Boys, as the Americans called us—achieved the objective its leader had set.

Bunny had prophesied that exactly a hundred days would be needed for the crossing of the continent.

We completed the journey in ninety-nine days.

You could hardly argue the toss with a man whose calculations had such slide-rule exactitude.

CHAPTER XI

Luxury Cruise

EARLY spring in London was a pleasant change from the February pack ice, but I had little time to enjoy the social round, for soon after *Theron*'s return I was despatched to New Zealand for a public relations tour with the idea of portraying to the public that the two ends of the expedition, Fuchs's and Hillary's, were in fact a single operational entity.

Ed, who had had his fill of public talking, was now busy with equipment problems and a training programme. During my stay I also flew around taking pictures of areas where the pre-Antarctic rehearsals of the New Zealand party could be performed.

By the end of June, however, the London organization was calling, and I flew back to England (over the *North* Polar route) to help with the last stages of planning before we again set sail for Shackleton Base in November.

On several occasions I went with Bunny Fuchs and David Stratton to the BBC, where we made our first contacts by radio with Ken Blaiklock and his seven companions of the advance party. They told of various troubles, especially of how slowly the building of the hut progressed (and of the stores they had lost), but although it was clear they were having no easy time of it, we in London got no real notion of the appalling conditions under which they lived and laboured.

Magga Dan, our new ship, was a Danish vessel specially built to withstand the pressure of ice. Ours was to be her maiden voyage, and at 1,800 tons she was twice the tonnage of *Theron*; she was also fatter, stronger, more powerful, more spacious, and a lot more comfortable.

In mid-November, exactly a year since *Theron*'s 1955 departure, *Magga Dan* was due to sail. Zero hour was eleven o'clock in the morning; the previous day I placed my belongings aboard, and we all met the Queen, our expedition patron, who inspected the ship and said good-bye before we left.

After a fitful night I drove slowly through London, went into St. James's Park and walked by the lake where the ducks stood forlornly on a thin layer of ice; the English winter was obviously going to be a cold one, and I laughed to myself as I thought of our Antarctic summer impending.

I knew that *Magga Dan* would be late in leaving so I walked and pondered on the outcome of the voyage. Would we really get across? Anyway, if we could only reach the Pole I would be satisfied . . . two years was a long time . . . but then again it was a short time in which to make the first crossing of a new continent . . . with any sort of luck we *would* cross . . . but I could not imagine in any detail what it would be like . . . perhaps the mountains would be impassable . . . perhaps only the dogs could get through . . . if so I wanted to be with the dog teams. . . .

A glimpse of orange sun could be seen through the London fog, Big Ben was hidden behind scaffold poles and I did not see the time clearly, but it was very near eleven. The ship would be crowded with people. Saying good-bye is not much fun. For those reasons I did not hurry.

I sauntered on to the wharf to find the expected great crowd milling around the dockside, and suddenly discovered that the decks were already cleared of people and the gangway had been taken inboard. I had to leap on a bollard and then jump across the gap to the well-deck, scrambling on top of a mountain of petrol drums. I was quite wrong about the ship being late, and it was exactly eleven o'clock when *Magga Dan* slid away from her moorings—in every sense I had almost missed the boat.

It was soon plain that the *Magga* was not to be the easy-going, darting vessel that *Theron* proved to be. All who made the *Theron* voyage told nostalgic tales and recalled the exploits of Harold Marø and his men. In *Theron* we were members of the crew; in the *Magga* we were passengers, and our cabins were of a better class than those of many a passenger liner.

With her propeller of variable pitch, her direction controlled by electronic gyroscopes, nobody stood at 'the wheel'. A gleaming pillar-box red, *Magga Dan* hardly had a personality of her own, we thought, as she rolled south with her crew showing an almost antiseptic disdain of the problems ahead.

From London to Madeira and Montevideo and across the stormy Atlantic to lonely South Georgia, where we arrived on a Monday morning, the 17th December, in the cold and pouring rain. Our Trans-Antarctic party shared the ship with a Royal Society group who were to occupy the IGY base which had been built at Halley Bay.

It was not until the *Magga* sailed from South Georgia on the 20th December that I had the surge of feeling that the expedition had truly begun. For the second time we were going into the unpredictable Weddell Sea, intending now to drive across the continent and sail away from the other side . . . my imagination ran out of control at the prospect and I felt disappointed and annoyed that the others were not burnt by the same flame. Bunny always amazed me by his calm, phlegmatic acceptance of his own brain-child. I wanted to see some sign of excitement, some light of inspiration, some fervour, some temperament. Many a time I was carried away by the magnitude and magnificence of the task, even frightened by it, and I wanted this feeling shared and talked about, but it never was.

We cleared the headland and steamed westwards through

calm water with the glaciers and mountains of the island leaping up into the clouds. The mountains were as tantalizing as ever, and seeing South Georgia again did not lessen its majesty.

In the late afternoon we came abreast of the Clerke rocks, an isolated group jutting sharply from the sea. They had never been visited and little information was given in *The Antarctic Pilot*. Earlier in the year, *Theron* had passed close to these brick-red rocks and Bunny and David Stratton were keen to attempt a landing, for geology and bird studies, but the approach was hazardous because of rough seas.

We slowed to half speed and crept in really close with the echo sounder and radar recording; less than a mile from the rocks the depth was some fifty-five fathoms. This time the conditions appeared ideal, with a low long swell pouring water over the lower rocks. Sea birds wheeled and cried.

A landing would have been exciting, and Bunny was keen to make one, but the captain decided against stopping; there were six large icebergs in sight—one stranded on the rocks and signs of many more to the south.

During the night heavy seas tossed the ship, and in the morning the captain altered course to safeguard the aircraft on deck. At eleven o'clock the ship suddenly went into an almighty roll; books, boots, bags and everything loose in the cabin were swept across, crashed and were hurled back again. Something must have happened to cause a roll like that; it appeared that an inexperienced helmsman had allowed the ship to swing 'beam on' to the sea. The rudder of the cocooned Otter aircraft took a wave as the sea swept inboard, the cocoon sealing was split wide open and the whole stressed rudder was badly twisted. John Lewis was very tart about it and went around red-faced for some hours. He estimated that a week of repair work would be needed. Peter Weston quietly dismantled the whole rudder and rebuilt it in a small room in the fo'c'sle.

Two days before Christmas we entered the fringe of the pack

ice. *Magga*'s route was to be along the same track as *Theron*'s exit, and a ripple of excitement ran through us—even Bunny was frisking about in a jubilant mood. Ice fever is much more violent than land fever.

Southern Thule of the South Sandwich Islands lay fifteen miles away on the port side. We steered a little south of east with heavy pack on the skyline to the south-west. An air of tension was developing because the decision was soon to be made on exactly where the *Magga* should turn and enter the maze. Bunny was continually scanning the southern horizon with binoculars; the captain sat in the crow's-nest, which was a glassed-in control box at the top of the mast, and steered the ship further east. There was a certain strain arising from the division of responsibility, for Bunny had once before had a terrible fight with the ice of this sea, did not want to repeat it but was determined at all costs to get through—while the captain was concerned to take his ship where he thought he could get through with maximum safety. Captain Petersen knew the ways of ice, but how *much* did he know, we wondered, and how would his new ship with its unusual modern controls react in the heavy pack of the Weddell Sea? Petersen was a big, silent man who often appeared to be surly; he was certainly hard to get to know, unlike *Theron*'s Harold Marø who was our *beau idéal* of an ice skipper.

During the afternoon our attention was diverted when Ralph Lenton called the ship from Shackleton. The first radio telephone contact with the base came through loud and clear. We talked for an hour and a quarter, asking about their living conditions and the state of the sea ice. Ken Blaiklock and Rainer Goldsmith were away from the base exploring inland and were expected back in six days' time . . . Ken had reached the foot of the Theron mountains and was bringing back rock samples . . . the temperature in the hut, in which they had no heating stove, had gone above freezing-point for the first time. . . . It was good to hear them talking after their year of isolated hardship. It was also clear that the advance party had suffered far more than we suspected.

Roy Homard spoke to David Pratt of his vehicle problems, which were many. They were now short of seals for dog food, they said, and asked us to collect as many as we could. The session ended when they had used the meagre ration of paraffin which ran their electrical generator.

Two hours later we came close to a huge iceberg lying in what appeared to be a perfectly still sea. It was decided to put Geoff Pratt on to this to try making a gravity measurement with his gravimeter. I went 'ashore' with him, over the ship's prow and sliding down a rope on to an ice ledge.

Magga Dan backed away, we climbed to the top of the berg and sat alone in the middle of the Weddell Sea. I always marvelled at the gravimeter, which looks something like a quart Thermos flask, costs about £3,500 and is so sensitive it can record the movement of the earth near the seashore when the tide is out and when the tide is in. The change in the weight of the water alters the gravitational pull and presses the land 'up' when the tide is full; the gravimeter can accurately measure this otherwise invisible motion.

Even though the huge berg on which we stood appeared to be solid and still, the sensitive gravimeter found that it was slowly rocking to and fro—about one-tenth of an inch, which was enough to make a reading impracticable. We called the ship back after an hour and continued south and east in very open pack ice.

Everybody crowded on deck to watch the *Magga*'s christening in the ice. It began with an area of pack that could not easily be skirted, so Captain Petersen drove straight for it. *Magga* slowed cautiously, glided up to the loose pack and slid her nose into the first ice, cutting through silently like a big cheese knife. Then came a bump and a shudder as we hit and smashed a big floe some ten feet thick. Red paint stains appeared dramatically on the bursting ice and two seals who were rudely wakened from their sleep on the floe slid quickly into the water. We all hung over the bow chattering like schoolboys on an excursion.

In the ice under Petersen's hand the *Magga* was superb. The variable-pitch propeller gave a control which was fascinating. Instead of backing and charging in frenzied bursts she pushed, barged and nudged forward at a steady unhurried pace. For two days we pushed through the ice-fields, the ship cutting her way with tremendous power. The hope was that we would outflank the area that had caught *Theron* the previous year.

On the 24th December we celebrated a Danish Christmas, which began in the afternoon with a visit from Father Christmas, the captain, bringing gifts. With a large sack and a benevolent word for all he distributed parcels, mine being a beautiful Royal Copenhagen china dish. The meal began with rice pudding in which was buried a single lucky almond. Then came goose, stuffed with prunes, in enormous helpings washed down with madeira that had been given to David Stratton— rare old vintages, two bottles of 1874 and two of 1910. We all had a taste and kept a bottle of each intact for the midwinter party at Shackleton.

The ship had stopped for the Christmas dinner and lay still in the ice. About midnight Bunny suggested to Geoff that a gravity measurement might be possible in the absolutely still ice. Geoff and I went over the side again by sliding down a rope from the bow, landing as fairy-like as possible and tiptoeing towards the centre. The ship was all lit up and throbbed with the sounds of revelry. On the ice a light of the intensity of early dusk gave the impression of night, but enough light suffused to see a great distance, and colours in the water and ice took on a velvet lustre.

Geoff found that the floe was moving up and down about one-fortieth of an inch and this was about twenty-five times too great for him to be able to take a reading, so we came aboard again. It seemed a bizarre occupation for Christmas night, jumping on an iceberg in the blue-black water of a dead still sea to see if you could measure a movement of one-fortieth of an inch.

Through Christmas Day and Boxing Day my cameras were kept running almost continuously, for a brilliant sun caused superbly photogenic shadows. David Stratton lowered me over the bow in a rope sling from where I went on filming while the ship smashed through the ice. For over an hour I swung within five feet of the bursting ice, vaguely conscious of being with, but not quite part of, the ship. It was bitterly cold but I felt the discomfort was worth while.

At midday on Boxing Day the ice-fields became extremely close and thick and it was decided to find a pool and fly an ice reconnaissance. The Auster rudder, which had been damaged, was now repaired, and the aeroplane was launched with John Lewis and Bill Pedersen, the first mate, as observer. They took off into perfect conditions and were back within the hour having found easier ice to the east. Quite quickly the ice became thinner and we made a hundred miles.

Next day we crossed the Antarctic Circle—for months to come the sun would not settle below the horizon. Progress was still good although the ice cover was now thicker and heavy— nearly ten-tenths cover, which means there was no water in sight. The ship ground forward, smashing everything at a steady walking pace. Both the captain and first mate proved excellent ice men and took it in turn to keep the ship thrusting forward twenty-four hours a day.

Still further east of our position was *Tottan*, a smaller vessel, taking further supplies to Halley Bay. She entered the ice some days behind us and by using our information was trying, as in the previous year, to outflank us and arrive first. There was considerable rivalry between the two captains and this put a keener edge on the decisions made to turn this way or that, decisions that had to be made almost instantly in the crow's-nest.

For the second time we talked with Shackleton Base. Ken

Blaiklock and Rainer Goldsmith had returned from their sledge journey to the Theron mountains and Ken gave a vivid account. The route for over a hundred miles seemed to be straight-forward over level ice shelf. The dogs ran well. The mountains, although 4,000 feet high, should be crossable—the summer days were sunny—and hot, which meant the temperature came *nearly* up to freezing-point.

Hopes were high the next morning when at nine o'clock the ship entered open water. A wide lead stretched away to the south. At eleven o'clock the captain switched on the automatic steering and we drove on past many icebergs. A southerly wind of over fifty knots whipped the crest off the light choppy sea. At lunch Bunny was bubbling with joy and the captain laughed and joked at the surprise of sailing south so easily.

But in the evening we came to a dead stop. Ahead and all around us except for our entry lead lay heavy pressure ice in which were embedded thirty-five huge icebergs. The visibility was deteriorating and the wind going down. Into this Gordon Haslop and the mate took off on another aerial reconnaissance.

Gordon investigated three leads in bad visibility, then turned and found his way back to the ship. We made an attempt along one lead and a few hours later we were stopped. The ice was heavily buckled and twisted by the windy day and we could not see more than five hundred yards.

By next morning we had not shifted. Over breakfast the captain sat in gloom, Bunny looked preoccupied and equally depressed.

At the end of breakfast the captain exploded a bombshell. Part of the gyroscope mechanism had gone wrong and all the compass readings had been fifteen degrees off true for five days. He even wondered if during the Christmas revels some idiot had thrown the vital electric switch for a few moments.

The ship was now eighty-seven miles west of her estimated position—in fact nearly into the worst of the ice which had caught *Theron* the first year. This was a galling reverse. We turned on our tracks to try to get away east.

Changes in the ice happen with staggering swiftness, without even appearing to happen. An hour after breakfast *Magga Dan* was trying to smash through hard, pressing ice, where the previous day there had been open sea. The ship began to back and charge. Standing about became impossible and we braced ourselves against the shocks. The bow rose ten feet as the ship reared up and then smashed down with her immense weight.

The gloom descended on everyone. Chart room and bridge were no longer buzzing with the laughter and banter of the day before. Petersen worked in the crow's-nest searching for a way out of the *impasse*, all the time torn between anger at the mistake which made him hurl the ship at the ice and chagrin at the news that *Tottan* was catching us to the east. The tension and the movements of the ship grew hourly more like the tense days in *Theron*.

Round about midnight, after a particularly vicious charge, the ship was unable to back out, the grip of the broken ice along the sides being too tight. For several hours we worked over the side digging and poling away the ice—the same old pattern as with *Theron*, removing great lumps jammed near the stern and freeing the ship sufficiently to allow her to 'wag her tail' by using the rudder. We did not break free till five o'clock in the morning.

I saw the New Year in from the crow's-nest where I spent four hours with the first mate. The captain handed over with the warning, 'Be careful now—go easy and *don't get stuck*.' It was an eerie and interesting four hours. From high in the crow's-nest one gets a sensation of being almost divorced from the ship. No sound could be heard from the engines and only occasionally the grinding and smashing of the ice reached the sealed, heated box at the masthead.

The mate fought his way north through pressure pack ice. *Tottan* had passed us and reported her position further east.

On the 2nd January we reached a small pool of clear water with new ice already beginning to form on the surface. Around the edge of the pool the sea was frozen into flowery patterns, standing up like clusters of white moss.

John Lewis flew from the pool with the mate as observer, and twenty miles to our east he found *Tottan* stopped by heavy ice. But fifteen miles away John also found open water under clear sunny skies. He directed both ships towards it—and these were our last hours in the ice.

For me they were busy hours. The sun at midnight lit up the pack with unbelievable shades of pink. I spent hours filming the shapes that were drenched in this liquid colour.

We sailed into the open water and Antarctica was in view, the coastal sea a shining blue like the Mediterranean.

On the 4th we reached Halley Bay, where we anchored against the ice behind diminutive *Tottan*, who had beaten us in the race by just a few hours.

CHAPTER XII

Cold Snap

WHILE we were approaching the continent from the Atlantic, Ed Hillary and the New Zealand support party were coming from the Pacific. The two sides of the expedition struck Antarctica on the same day, 4th January, and as soon as he arrived Ed sent us a message to say he had landed.

Bunny's reply, apt though somewhat thin for such an occasion, was: SNAP. In this fashion the two sides were linked.

After a week of unloading at Halley Bay we were still two hundred and fifty miles from the men at Shackleton Base, and though *Magga* would be sailing there in the next twenty-four hours Bunny did not want to wait any longer before re-uniting us with the advance party. To save time, and especially to hurry a few luxury supplies like fresh meat, fruit, bread, a bag of coal, and mail, he decided to fly there in the Otter. John Lewis was the pilot, and I went with them to film the scenery as well as the first reunion.

We took off in rather cloudy weather, heading south along the coast, keeping underneath the cloud. But as we went further the cloud got lower and a good deal of the time we were at three hundred feet, for at least a quarter of an hour pressed down to as low as a hundred feet. The windows iced over with our breath . . . I could see seals when I scraped myself a peephole with my knife. We were at the level of the tops of the ice-

125

bergs, winding in and out of them along the coast—an exciting variety of hedge-hopping.

After a while we ran into limitless blue sky—almost indigo, like high-altitude sky over Everest and a wonderful contrast to the ground view of white ice. We made altitude, the radio conditions improved, and at last we made contact with Shackleton, and Taffy Williams, the radio operator there, came through loud and clear; there was a lot of banter when John Lewis told him we were carrying cans of beer.

After two hours' flying John Lewis gave us the thumbs-up signal. He had spotted the base hut, and presently we could distinguish the specks on the ice shelf. We flew in over the base, John making a couple of circuits for me so that I could film. As we circled all the boys below came out to wave and watch. From the air the place looked incredibly small—a good deal of the stores were either underground or hidden by snow, and it looked a fantastic place for eight men to have spent the winter. The hut was now erected, but it too was buried, with only the roof visible.

We landed on the air strip they had prepared for us, I leapt out with my three cameras and filmed the meeting between Bunny and the advance party.

For Blaiklock and the others this was just a normal day; for us the temperature and cold south wind were shrivelling. We dived for the hut thinking we would get warmth and protection, but it was in fact colder in than outside. The hut had no heating because all the coal had been lost in a great March storm which had blighted their first weeks the previous year.

We carried in our gifts from the outer world with some ceremony—the bag of coal, fresh bread from the ship, fresh meat, apples, oranges, bananas. Then came a surprise. Ken led us into their kitchen, which was small and fairly warm, where they had laid out a feast of welcome. They had baked enormous cakes, home-made biscuits, buns of all sorts, a cottage loaf which was far better than those we brought. All were baked in an oil-drum stove which Roy Homard had made.

We all had a three-course meal finishing with sugared dough cakes, more succulent even than doughnuts, a South African speciality which Hannes had cooked. I was tremendously impressed by the initiative and enthusiasm of all the preparations, and the results made our meals on the ship seem relatively dull. The pathetic aspect of the party's outward appearance was somehow invested with a triumphant dignity by the warmth and efficiency of this welcoming reception. Everyone had had a haircut and shaved off his beard for the occasion.

We handed over the large bag of mail from home—the first letters they had received for a year. Silence fell and each man took himself into a quiet corner with his pile of correspondence. Almost the first letter Roy Homard opened contained an invitation to join another expedition when this one ended. 'Not bloody likely,' said Roy, then adding, 'but I suppose when I've been home a few months I'll be a fool again and probably say Yes.'

He went on reading. So did the others, and I watched them as they sat or sprawled surrounded by the torn envelopes and sheaves of news, gossip and affection from wherever home was.

Their clothing, greasy from constant wear and work, was patched everywhere. Their faces were scaly and lined. Their hands, etched deep with grime, were calloused. Nobody had bathed or even washed much during the year because of the fuel shortage.

Later in the evening and well into the night as we lay in our sleeping-bags (after *Magga*'s central heating it was icy cold and I took off only my boots) I listened while Ralph, Roy, Hannes and Ken told the stories, or some of them, that summed up the hard year through which they had fought to keep their slippery foothold on the continent. In March 1956, only a few weeks after *Theron* left them, ten days of wind and storm swamped the hut frame to the eaves with hundreds of tons of snow. Worse still, the sea ice broke up, taking most of their stores out to sea. They lost all their coal and petrol, a boat, a tractor and much other equipment. They were left with no heating for the winter. At first the eight men were quite numbed by this blow. Dumbfounded, they went to the hut site to sit. Ken said he brewed a cup of tea and they talked about it. The party's confidence was already beginning to quake. Could they survive? Could they eke out the stores they had and get through a winter of unknown severity in tents with no heating? They felt they had been marooned on the continent.

A suggestion was made that they try to make their way overland to the Argentinian base. After the first shock Ken went round carefully assessing the stores they had earlier brought to the hut site. He had chosen wisely and transported a small selection of all that was vital. If they rationed paraffin carefully —for cooking only—they could survive, he said.

The stock of seal-meat for the dogs had gone and this would mean strict rationing for the dogs until more seals could be caught when the sun returned. But they themselves had ample food. The hut lay in pieces around them and erecting it was their first task. It took them seven months to complete it.

The hut was their Achilles' heel. Designed by a bridge builder it could withstand a load of more than three hundred tons on roof or walls. Every bolt-hole was already drilled and in theory the prefabricated sections could easily be assembled. The trouble was that not everything in Antarctica was quite as it seems to be on a plumb floor, and when they got down to the task of erection, nothing—or nearly nothing—would fit with the easy, trouble-free rapidity envisaged in London. Then came the March storm. Before long they were digging the partially built structure free from nearly two hundred tons of snow. When that was practically cleared the wind blew up more fiercely than ever and flung the snow back at them, to be dug away once more. They were having to dig, too, for every scrap of hut material they needed, for it was being constantly buried in deep drifts.

They passed the winter in tents, a grim, uncomfortable

experience with the sun totally set during April so that for the next four months they would have a more or less continuous darkness. Even in the dark, however, they continued building their hut, using small Tilley lanterns to light the working hours. They were also continually digging their tents out from the drift, and shifted them six times in the four winter months to keep them on the surface. Little of their time could be devoted to actual building, since most days went in digging, shifting snow, moving away from the weather. Each day the party met and ate their meals inside a Sno-Cat crate twenty feet long, ten feet wide and eight feet high.

Throughout their year the eight were under constant strain, and there were substantial problems of mental adjustment and nervous tension to overcome. Against this background there were some odd happenings. Most striking of all was their 'ghost story', an incident in the depth of winter. Out on the ice they saw a light moving, and all went to look. Then two of the party —Ralph and Ken, two men who had spent a good many years in the Antarctic—were absolutely convinced that the light indicated a party of strangers on the ice two miles away. They thought they may have been Argentinians who had a base further along the coast. This may be a lost Argentinian group, they argued.

A powerful paraffin lantern was lit. Ralph and Ken set off with it to meet the moving light.

They walked across the ice with the mysterious light ahead of them. A mile or more and still the light was ahead.

As they went inland from the base, imperceptible undulations in the ice occurred, hummocks that measured ten or twelve feet from trough to crest. Down in each trough they saw no light, and reaching each crest the light would reappear.

This happened a few times—and then the light disappeared altogether.

The two men plodded on, feeling the whole thing was distinctly odd. A mile and a half from the base they decided they had had enough and turned to find their way back to the snow-covered tents and the chilly framework of their hut.

Now an odder thing happened. The six men left working on the hut site had become convinced that 'foreign' visitors were returning. When the lantern approached the base they grew excited and went out to meet it.

On meeting only Ken and Ralph they were completely deflated. Attention had been so riveted on encountering someone new that they all forgot their two colleagues existed. The dream was shattered. They were alone, with nothing and no one to help them.

At another, earlier stage Hannes had hallucinations. He was very shaken by the fact that *Theron* disappeared and that they were left on the ice when he was not expecting it. He knew it was going to happen but didn't clearly anticipate it. Hannes, one of the most likeable of men, couldn't anticipate much, anyway—he was also that sort of character. He always sat on a tractor and drove it across the ice as if he were ploughing a tract of land on the veldt, and was incapable of anticipating a crevasse. We used to say he sat so solidly that if he fell through a crevasse he would hit the bottom with a crash, still in his seat and still not registering that the fall had taken place; he would then have stepped off his tractor, scratched his head and said: 'Hm—crevasse!'

And when it came to anticipating *Theron*'s departure it was the same story—he could not imagine it.

Soon afterwards he began looking at icebergs and believing they were ships. He would cry out: 'A ship! A ship!' The others acidly told him: 'There's no bloody ship, Hannes—you'll have to get on without it.' From that moment he took to walking from the base out of earshot, pointing away to the sea and shouting to himself: 'A ship! A ship!'

Eventually the advance party got over such tensions and straightened themselves out. Listening to their stories it was clear that they had undergone a profound experience.

Magga Dan reached Shackleton the day after our arrival by air, unloaded and sailed away at the end of January. As she moved off, at the precise hour and minute that the captain said he would leave, we felt no regrets; it was not that we had no kinship with *Magga* and her crew, but our thoughts were now rapidly turning to the yet more exciting problems of exploring the interior, away from the sea and pack ice we knew so well.

A cold wind blew into our faces as we drove back to the hut site from the sea. Ken and David Stratton had brought down a dog team and these set off at a wild pace. We chased them hard with the Sno-Cat and the Muskeg but the huskies were much faster over the rough ice.

With the ship gone, we celebrated our real establishment with mugs of tea. For the first time the expedition seemed to have come together as a community and there was a universal feeling of coherent unity. We spent the day cleaning the hut surroundings and depositing unused timber in a well-marked dump. Nothing was wasted.

The base was stretched all round the hut. A quarter of a mile away the long lines of fuel drums lay end to end, a perfect marker from the air. Beyond the fuel dump stood the Otter and Auster ready and eager for flying.

'Well, all we have to do now,' somebody was heard murmuring, 'is cross the bloody continent.' True enough, I thought, as I looked at the map on the wall and reflected on the differences between the two Poles. . . .

North Pole—over the sea and surrounded by continents. South Pole—over a continent and surrounded by oceans. An ice-covered continent as big as the whole of the United States and Europe together. *All we had to do was cross.* . . .

CHAPTER XIII

A House in the Country

Shackleton Base, Jan. 27, 1957
My dear Ann:

The time has come to break the thread of letters. It is sad that I can't send you any more, because the interesting days are just starting, with the base well established, with everything more or less in order to move inland once we have the route decided.

I have been lucky to be in the spearhead of the advance. Have been with each of the three long flights inland, to photograph and assess the possibilities of the route. We had hoped, when we flew yesterday, finally to settle the question of the route to Depot 300, or South Ice. Yesterday we took off with a long-range tank filled, giving us 15 hours' duration in the air. We covered the 125 miles across to the Theron Mountains and crossed these to find cloud lying thickly over the most important part of the route. We reluctantly turned back. It would have been good to have sent home, with the ship, news and pictures of the route into South Ice and then you would have known as much of the way ahead as we will know until next November.

Settling in has been hard work but great fun. This is so different from the Himalayan journeys. There is not as much time to read and write at the end of the day. The days are longer and there is no time when one can find a shady—or a sunny—spot on a mossy bank and look up at the sky. The temperature on a good day like today is $+5°F$ or $+10°F$ with a quiet wind from the south.

Three days from now I have to take my turn as cook. What would *you* do for sixteen hungry men? David Stratton has started with a fine roast of lamb, with apple puddings, natty custards and trimmings which seem unsurpassable. It's a pity I have to follow him. I must do a quiet hour over the cookery book. There is no 'Alimentation' or 'Madame's' at the water-front for us to drive to or stand dreaming whether we'll buy artichokes or rice, no fat brown onions hanging from the ceiling. Instead it's a snow-covered box with an index number which means beans or spaghetti or tongue, all in tins.

The shortage of water is the main bind. Everything has to be dug out, carried in and melted and that is a great bore. The library is excellent—so valuable that I hope a lot of it is shipped out at the end of this year.

From the observations of the ice cleavages I should say that the days of Shackleton Base are numbered in months and years. It's obvious that within a year or two—maybe more, maybe less—the whole corner on which we live is going to cleave right away from the parent ice shelf behind—and go out as a huge iceberg.

I haven't heard the world news for some weeks now and I wonder what has happened in Hungary, in Suez, in England with the petrol rationing. I know Anthony Eden has resigned. Oddly enough the most pleasant memory I have of England is in the big calendar you bought for me in Wigmore Street. The first is a colour picture—a simply beautiful shot of the winter sunshine in St. James's Park with the ducks sitting on the frozen pond. The next, and I couldn't help looking before the time, is February with a warm sunny shot of Snowdon from the tarns.

I have been in a wonderfully dreamy mood, having come

down to a farewell party on the ship. Picture me with a most fragrant cigar and a glass of fine champagne with the others quietly reading *Punch* and preparing for a boisterous final night. It's not only the cigar and champagne that make me reflective but I am very contented here—I was thinking that only this morning as I sat over the icy petrol drum that serves as our lavatory. First, the flights inland, and now being face to face with the real journey ahead. . . . I'm much happier about it than I was in London. Certainly it will be hard—but exciting, and the big thing is that I think it really is possible.

I have not thought much about the infinities of life, the reasons why we're alive and where we go. All I know is that I should like to live to be a mellow, whimsical century (at least), and that all of it is etched deep with things like ducks in the park in the winter cold, hailstorms slashing over Pyrenean passes, hock in a Soho restaurant, coffee in the Brompton Road, morning creeping over the vineyards of Banyuls, sunset on the Broads, haddocks in the Welsh lakes and Mozart in a warm room. Making mistakes on mountains or with the journey across Antarctica doesn't really appeal at all—and although there are fascinating memories of these journeys in my mind's eye, I should not like to die doing it.

The moments of beauty here are many, and unless they can be experienced they seem quite uncommunicatable (funny word, that—it must be the drink). I am now looking forward to the autumn, because the sun will set. I have missed that daily occurrence here, and when it does happen there will be colours aplenty. I wonder if you are going away on a skiing holiday—if so you will know and experience some small part of the crisp sparkling world in which we are living now.

It may sound silly but the moments of great excitement have always hit me as we fasten our seat-belts and start the fast take-off run in the Otter on our inland flights. The sun has always been brilliant and the snow sparkling and cold. We know we are going south to see something new, and as I check the settings on the three cameras I have in my lap I almost want to yell with excitement—and even lean over and pinch the pilot's leg. An odd fact, but true, the snow here does not fall in wonderful star-shaped patterns as in England, but in little needles of hexagonal columns. This Hal Lister tells me is the change of air temperature and humidity—they are not the same—and perhaps not as beautiful until they go under a microscope.

In future flights I think I will take my diary with me and write as we fly. Sorry I'm not saying much, but I've enjoyed rattling on like this. My cigar is ending—my champagne is nearly done and I'm full of misty goodwill towards all the friends in London. Please give my love. . . .

Yours,
George.

Cigars and champagne apart, it was true that the inland flights, the first days of probing from Shackleton Base, were full of excitement. This was to some extent due to the presence of John Lewis at the controls, for John always flew the Otter as if the aircraft were an avenging Spitfire. The contrast between him and Gordon Haslop was strong and interesting to observe in action.

Gordon flew with the steadiness of a veteran transport pilot; he climbed into the cabin of the aircraft, carefully strapped himself in, wearing his shining bone dome and sun vizor; always went through his cockpit drill, then rechecked it; opened up the throttle, broke the plane free of the ice bed and took off with a steady copybook run; left the snow gaining height at a steady rate, turned and set course over the base; all as if he were taking a ton of coal into Berlin, as indeed he took many tons during the crisis there.

Whereas we never needed to be told when John, the former young Battle of Britain ace, was flying. He would climb aboard, scorning to strap himself in, and wore an old leather helmet which he kept for sentimental reasons.

For his take-off, he 'gunned up' the motors violently, checked through rapidly, gave a nod to himself, then turned to shout a boyish 'Whacko Blue, we're off'—and break the skis free. A take-off was always a 'scramble'.

Once in the air, the moment he left the snow, whether we had a load or not, he immediately put the plane into a turning climb and without fail 'beat-up' the base or any figure walking below him. With whips and turns he then flashed on his way, flying, he said, by the seat of his pants. John boomed and blustered and loved every minute he spent in the air. Gordon was neat, meticulous, efficient, ironed his clothes (the only man among us who did) and kept everything spotless whenever he was on kitchen duties. By markedly different routes the two men reached the same excellent standard of flying.

Broken, for a while, was the thread of letters to friends in a dozen parts of the world, but I went on with my diary. . . .

Shackleton, Feb. 1, 1957

The week seems to have flicked by with the speed of 24 hours. Every day sees new things completed and now we are on the brink of an exciting plan: the establishment of Depot 300.

It is hoped for the Otter to fly on Sunday for Depot 300 which will be about 250 air miles and 300 ground miles from Shackleton. This decision was made only last night and means a well-nigh impossible amount of preparation to be completed tomorrow. The first party to go in will be Hal Lister, Jon Stephenson (both are to stay the winter there) with Ken Blaiklock and me to help start the building programme.

For the last five days we have been all over the place covering outside huts with Ruberoid (bituminous felt), sealing cracks with Bostik and felt strips, putting in lighting, fixing a work bench into the workshop. Ruberoiding was a cold job which

Taffy Williams

John Lewis

Allan Rogers

Ralph Lenton

Peter Weston

Geoff Pratt

Gordon Haslop

Jon Stephenson

Jon Stephenson and I did for three days. We became very adept at handling short fat nails with long-nosed pincers—it was too cold to work with bare fingers.

Every day our beards ice up—especially under the nose, but this doesn't seem to worry us and is better than being clean shaven.

Saturday, Feb. 2.

Afraid we are all very tired, rushing with loads of hut material to be flown to South Ice. Still 101 things to prepare and still not certain if we will get away tomorrow.

Today Hal Lister, Jon Stephenson and I worked on the hut for South Ice, putting the various pieces into 2,000-lb. loads for the aircraft to lift. There will be five or six hut loads and then fuel and food; altogether about 16 loads are expected to be flown in—enough for a wintering party of three. Having another discussion tonight about our requirements. Nearly asleep on my feet.

Monday, Feb. 4.

I have made many take-off runs in aircraft and always find the experience exciting. Today was perhaps the best yet. It was a great thrill when, half an hour ago, the heavily-loaded Otter waddled round on to the snow path and prepared for the first flight to South Ice, Depot 300. At the starting-point John Lewis checked everything with special care as our next landing is to be at 6,000 feet—three hundred miles inland on an unknown surface in unknown wind conditions.

The checks done, he opened the throttle and the plane came unstuck from its frozen position and moved forward a yard or two. John eased back the throttle, turned to us three, lying on the piles of skis, sleeping-bags, food, survey theodolites, shovels, wireless and tents which fill the aircraft. We gave him the thumbs up. We lurched forward, faster and faster. The petrol dump flashed by with all the boys standing on the drums waving as we became airborne. It was just here that I felt the tremendous thrill—a mixture of so many feelings as we made our departure on the first move across the continent.

The sea, smoking with vapour from air temperature changes, was covered with strips of dull new ice; elsewhere it was blue. Jon and Hal, who won't see it again until we reach the other side of the continent, looked back with some feeling as we turned our course inland.

12.30 p.m.: We are going in to land, running low to look at the surface with little drift patterns which look as if there are three strong prevailing winds. . . .

Now 30 feet above it and it looks good. . . .

Here we go. . . .

John has fired a brown smoke puff with the Very pistol to watch the wind drift, which is from south-east. . . .

1.46: Going in now to touch down. . . .

Tuesday, Feb. 5.

South Ice 81°57′ *South.* . . . Our landing was perfect—with the heavy load and the altitude about 5,000 feet John kept plenty of motor revving as we crept down, bumped lightly and ski-ed to a stop.

We three in the back and Ken up front jumped down. Hal grabbed a shovel and began digging to see if the ground below was snow or ice. We looked around, amazed to find we were on a featureless desert without the view of the mountains we had seen 50 feet higher. We wondered whether to search for a site within view of the peaks but by this time we'd unloaded the aircraft. However, Ken and Hal got in and John taxied a couple of miles north and put them down—but they could only just see the very top of the nearest nunatak [a rocky mass surrounded by ice, often the spiky top of a buried mountain]. They ski-ed back and we decided to dig in and begin the hut site. The aircraft left us with our tents and our food, intending to return immediately about ten that night with the next load.

We began digging the foundations for the hut, which meant digging five feet down over the hut area of 19 feet by 18 feet.

At 9.15 we were to listen on our tiny radio for the return time of the Otter. We received nothing after listening for an hour. The hand-wound transmitter was frozen inside and the motor kept slipping, so we did not get through. Then we switched on *Sarah*, the radio direction finder for the aircraft—but no aircraft came. So we slept.

Wed., Feb. 6.

This morning at 9.30 tried again to make radio contact and failed. The day crept on, with the hole nearly full size, but our backs and arms bloody sore from the digging. The top three feet were easy going but the next two were very hard to break.

We have a Terylene tarpaulin but it is too small to cover the whole area—and drifting snow could fill the hole overnight. Until the aircraft arrives it seems no use enlarging the hole, so at 6 p.m. we covered the dug area and crept into our tents.

At 7 p.m. without any warning the aircraft roared low over the tents and we dashed out to receive it. I held up the red wind-sock to indicate the wind direction. John Lewis circled and touched down beautifully, and we then unloaded 2,400 lbs. of floor grillage, or base, and levelling beams.

Ralph Lenton was aboard; he came for several reasons—first, to try improving our wireless communications and also to advise us on setting-out the hut foundations. He produced bread which had been baked that morning, and the remains of a fine leg of mutton, now frozen stiff. Reason for the delayed flights was bad weather at Shackleton. We stacked the stores and crept to bed again.

Thursday, Feb. 7.

The third day of digging was the worst. Our arms ached and the hole was at its deepest, so the throwing of each shovelful was agony. By midday it was ready and big enough, and we drove in the first levelling pegs and set the levelling timbers. Finished by 5 p.m.

Today was colder, about zero F., with steady drift blown by a 20-knot wind. In the hole we were protected from the wind and used the tarpaulin to deflect the drift. The cloud thickened in the evening and the conditions were too bad for any aircraft to come in. We worked on and laid the expanded metal over the levelled timbers and filled and packed the whole area with snow. This will act as our firm hut foundation. On this we laid out the 21 aluminium H-shaped beams which will act as the hut grillage.

These beams were cut in half for easy handling and had to be joined by plates and bolts. Here was a mad bit of designing. Each beam was joined by using seven plates requiring twenty bolts of different sizes. Twenty-one beams and twenty bolts for each join was absolute hell in the cold. Had to use bare hands and we were all tired and cold at the end of the day. With an enormous spurt we finished this about 9.30 p.m., went to our tents, fed on pemmican, and slept.

I slept until the alarm awoke me at 3 a.m. as I am the met. man for these two days and we make observations every six hours round the clock, at nine and three o'clock, a.m. and p.m. It was awful getting out to read the thermometers, estimate the cloud and cloud formation, read the aneroid and record all this in the met. book. When I crept into the bags again I was fully awake.

Now it's 11 a.m. and we've stopped work, having progressed as far as we can go until the next airlift arrives. Perhaps it will come today—if not this weather will be wasted. Today is 'Good' . . . +5°F with 20-knot E. wind.

Friday, Feb. 8.

Yesterday was the anniversary of the date that *Theron* sailed away from Shackleton last year. At midday, after we had waited three or four hours with nothing to do, the Otter flashed in and landed with Gordon Haslop flying and Bunny coming to see progress. They brought the vital roof framework which was holding us up and a new wireless receiver (which had not been checked at Base and was found to be U/S, so we sent it back). They stayed for an hour and departed with intentions of flying again today. . . .

And now we have just received the fourth flight with John Lewis and Allan Rogers aboard. The plane was absolutely chock full of roof panels and door frames. They stayed half an hour and then rushed off as the aircraft hopes to make a second flight today.

The weather is as near perfect as it will be—it's a pleasure to be out. Sun is warm, sky cloudless, and a light breeze of five knots from the S.E. Temp. is +4°F.

We have now erected the aluminium framework and that makes the place look well on the way to being finished. Even so the bolting and screwing is a curse. So far we have put in 600 bolts, washers and nuts. Today we began on the floor panels which have to be felted on the edges and then cramped together with wire ropes. Tacking felt is done with tiny tacks and bare hands, and we're lucky it's such a nice day for it.

The wind is now getting stronger, and with lunch inside of us (cocoa and a slice of bread and cheese) we now go back for the long afternoon shift.

Saturday, Feb. 9.

Again we are waiting on the plane during the warmest, calmest period of the day. It's midday and we cannot proceed as the hopes of a double flight yesterday did not materialize.

Finished the floor panels, packed them with glass wool, and went on to felt the edges of the roof panels—but found the roof panels could not be placed as several vital pieces of timber have not yet arrived.

Fixed the centre struts in the main hut structure and braced all the frames with heavy cross timbers, all bolted in position with four bolts.

Stopped yesterday at 9 p.m. very cold and stiff. As we get hungry we get cold very rapidly. The temp. was −11°F with little wind and clear sky. But this morning was better. It was −9°F with practically no wind and I worked for a time in a shirt, with no jersey or anarak.

It is easy now to handle nails and tacks with bare hands as there is no wind and our hands have toughened amazingly fast. It was so warm this morning we hung up our sleeping-bags and the sheepskin mats on which we sleep; these dried out in the sun and now the tent looks fairly clean. The tents are quite different from climbing tents. In shape they are pyramid, seven feet high with four stout internal poles and each weighs 54 lbs. against the climbing tent's 14 lbs. The polar tent is heavyweight material that must last a couple of years against the two or three months of a Himalayan expedition.

Sunday, Feb. 10.

The four of us here get along very happily. Hal Lister is a most amusing character with a great attitude to life. His favourite saying when things go wrong . . . 'If mother knew this she'd try and buy me out.'

The hut was designed by a bridge architect and its strength is fantastic. Today Hal worked over the plans and discovered that a line of extra metal struts should have been put in at some earlier stage.

'We're only going to *live* in the hut,' he said, 'we're not trying to roll the bloody thing over.'

A most lasting design, but it seems silly to spend perhaps a fortnight putting together fiddly bits of fantastic strength and longevity when it is to be used for maybe eight months. The dimensions are only 16 feet by 16 feet. The framework consists of fifty iron girders with a line of centre struts and cross strutting in aluminium and *then* 4-inch by 2-inch wooden cross beams in between the metal frame. Over this go sixty roof and wall panels four inches thick, of stressed aluminium and plywood packed with glass wool. The directions for erecting cover six sheets of foolscap and the plans are on twelve sheets three feet square, with from five to eight plans per page. The final bit we all enjoyed. A footnote at the end said: 'It will probably be necessary to put some of the cupboard and furniture fittings into the hut *before* the wall panels as the door does not seem big enough.'

Anyway, as long as the good weather holds we are lucky; if it snows, or a heavy wind blows drift . . . we will have twenty tons of snow inside before the wall panels arrive from Shackleton.

Monday, Feb. 11.

Sunday afternoon went by digging and tunnelling—the weather stayed clear although the wind increased to 20 knots, blowing steady drift with the temp. at −2°F. As there was little to do until the aircraft returned Ken and Jon left at 1 p.m. to ski to the nearest rock nunatak, about six miles distant. Jon, the geologist, wanted to collect the rock specimens and see what was what. Ken wanted to fix a survey angle on the first range north of here, 26 miles away but out of sight from us. Ken has now fixed our latitude at 81° 56′ South, which puts us about 500 miles from the Pole.

Hal and I dug and tunnelled and discussed the disappointment we felt at the lack of flights and the slow progress on the hut. We cut the few sacks we had and found a few sticks of wood that could be spared and made these into a cover for the eight-feet deep trench we dug. We placed the heavy hut door over the escape hole and tried to seal the cracks down against drift.

We stopped for a long brew at 6 p.m. which stretched until 7.30 when we reckoned Ken and Jon should arrive. By 8.30 there was no sign of them and we prepared a meal against the possibility of setting out to look for them. The met. had to be recorded at 9 p.m. and sent out on the damned hand-crank machine at 9.15. This we did (temp. −17°F.) and it proves to be a bitterly cold job, out in the wind, sitting on the snow using a rough morse key on your knees.

As we finished sending, Ken and Jon appeared on the skyline a mile away and came slowly in. They arrived with their faces covered with frost and very tired. They had ski-ed about fifteen miles. They found the rock, which was only a few feet high above the surface and lying to the north; because of this they nearly missed it. Around it the ground was broken by crevasses. Geologically it was most disappointing to find rock of no great character. This has made Jon more and more keen to reach the rock points of the 'nunatak range' 26 miles away.

The night was cold—with the onset of winter the temperature drops a little lower each night.

Today we have waited and waited for the aircraft to bring us hut supplies. The framework stands there stark and bare and we are working constantly with tarpaulin wind deflectors to keep the hut site free of drift.

We began to wonder what will be our moves if the days pass and the aircraft has to be presumed damaged or lost. But we have a plan: we shall wait until we have only ten days' food and fuel left, then set out to walk towards Shackleton, by which time a relief party on the ground should surely be reaching us. We also discussed the possibilities of making a sail, out of canvas, to assist the propulsion of the little Nansen sledge.

The wind was getting up in the afternoon, and at 4.15 when Ken and I were digging a tunnel for the future generating room, the aircraft arrived from Shackleton, landing with a precious load of roof and wall panels (16 of them, we need 40), and a 40-gallon drum of kerosene. Gordon Haslop was pilot with Geoffrey Pratt in for the ride, carrying his gravimeter to make local readings.

The reason for the long delay, they said, was a 30-knot

blizzard at Shackleton which hurled drift everywhere. Even so, everybody at Shackleton felt that *we* would have more than enough to do. This lack of reliable radio communication is an obstacle to the flying programme, for they always take off from Shackleton without knowing the weather conditions here. Our hand-wound transmitter is not getting through. Bad wireless communications are a curse, almost worse than no radio at all.

Gordon left at 5 p.m. with the intention of reloading and returning again by midnight. We worked happily on. Gone the clouds of despair about the thought of walking out, and we placed all the roof panels into place by 1 a.m. It was very cold, with strong wind and —12 degrees F.

Disappointed once again, working and waiting till midnight to find no aircraft returning. Turned in and slept.

Tuesday, Feb. 12.

Again searched the sky in vain for our flying hut supplies. Still no aircraft. After working late last night we lay in bed till 9 a.m. We all suffered from the cold today, which varied between —9°F and —15°F with a searing East wind.

My nose was frozen several times and I thawed it in my hands. Noses are a great nuisance in the cold because they dribble incessantly and this freezes in great ice knobs all round the moustache.

Today for the first time, in addition to long woollen combinations and thick woollen trousers with windproofs over them, with a thick shirt, two jerseys, and windproof jacket, *in addition* we all wore an oversuit of eiderdown jacket and pants or the same in nylon fur. Jon and I in eiderdowns were warmer than Ken and Hal in the fur.

We stopped at 9 p.m. with the temp. dropping steadily. The inside walls of the tents are beginning to ice over with condensation and outside cold. We had (Ken and I) a huge pemmican meal followed by a small but delightful tin of straw-

145

berries and then coffee with some Turkish delight that was given to me.

Wed., Feb. 13.

At 4.30 the sixth flight arrived. The day has been bad, with wind and cloud from the N.E. and we thought the aircraft would never get through. All very glad it did arrive. John Lewis and Taffy Williams were aboard. Taffy came to install the 'Ernest Turner' wireless transmitter and receiver, a far superior job, and Taffy contacted Ralph at Shackleton on radio telephone. Weather observations were exchanged. The aircraft took off at 8 p.m. leaving behind fuel and the remaining hut panels which we will now be able to put in place.

The weather at Shackleton was improving and with that prospect we hope to receive another load of supplies at 3 a.m. or thereabouts tomorrow.

Peter Weston's wife had a son, born yesterday.

Thursday, Feb. 14.

Expected flights did not arrive—again bad weather at Shackleton with cloud and snow. Here too we had our worst weather. Last night the wind increased to 30 knots and gusts of gale force, whipping with it clouds of drifting snow, which caused a whirling, seething cloud of drift about fifteen feet high. We spent the morning clearing piles of snow from around and in the hut, and changing the position of the wireless set; this we placed in the 30-feet snow tunnel where it is warmer and almost drift-free.

After lunch in this high wind and drift we placed the last wall in position and fixed the door frame. All of us were covered, inside and outside our clothes, with fine dustings of snow which get into everything.

Eyelashes froze together and had to be cleared every quarter of an hour or so, snow blocked up our noses and the dog fur on the anarak hood became clogged with snow and froze into our beards—very painful to remove. At 7 p.m. the last panel went into place and we escaped to our flapping tents.

Monday, Feb. 18.

Landed here at South Ice a fortnight ago today. Since then we have received only five further flights. For five days now the wind storm has raged over the camp. On Friday the drift piled high around the drift walls and buried them with five feet of snow. Drift soaked in through every crevice and piled a few hundredweight of snow inside the hut. We dug out the door from the drift outside and bolted this into place. On Saturday the wind screamed from the East, with drift forming higher and higher.

I was on met. observation again and getting up at 3 a.m. was hellish.

Whenever we grew too cold, fixing screws in ventilators or nailing on boards out in the wind, we dug galleries off the sides of the snow tunnel. The wind and drift continued and the wireless began to fade and give trouble. Last night the wind lulled for a while and we had hopes of a calm but this morning it was roaring at a steady 30 knots, hurling snow everywhere.

Disposing of the snow dug from the tunnels is now the biggest task. The temp. in the hut is generally lower than outside and we spend no time standing about. Inside the tent is the only warm drift-free place. If this weather continues I can't see how they can make enough flights to consolidate this position for the winter. We have only 25 days' supplies left now. It will be a great disappointment to Hal Lister if this base is not established—it would mean the end of his glaciological programme.

Just when hopes seem lowest the aircraft arrives. At the 4 p.m. wireless schedule with base, we heard the Otter had left and was trying to reach us. The wind and drift was still bad but occasionally the visibility lifted to 500 yards. At 5.45 we talked direct with Gordon and Ralph in the aircraft which was somewhere overhead, but we could not see them.

147

Sarah, our radar beacon, was switched on and this brought them to us, but the drift obscured everything for 20 feet above ground level. We set off four powerful flares, each of us running like demons placing the flares in line with the wind.

Gordon saw only one of these flares, turned to land and lost the camp again. The last I heard on the radio was—'Please fire rockets—I have lost your position again.'

I shouted to the others to fire rockets and dived back to the radio. Rockets swept up into the sky. I listened and called the aircraft and received nothing. I ran outside and looked and saw the others firing away in the murkiness.

Five minutes went by. As I was calling again, rather frantically, Jon Stephenson dashed in covered with ice and shouted, 'They're here, they've landed.' Outside 40 yards away I could just distinguish the blur of the aeroplane in the whirling drift.

It was a wonderful effort of Gordon's, setting down the loaded aeroplane blindly into the drift. He could not see the ground, merely flew in, cut the motor, made a guess—and guessed rightly. Once down he could not see the camp, taxied on his compass, then saw the rockets which led him in. So arrived our sixth load of supplies.

Wed., Feb. 20.

Suddenly I am reluctantly leaving South Ice behind. Today the aircraft made the 7th load flight (eighth trip—we were in the first) and landed at 4.30 with John Lewis and Bunny aboard.

After unloading Bunny asked me to pack up and return with this flight. Three men, he thought, were enough to complete the hut.

Hal Lister was in great spirits as he heard today that *his* wife has also borne a son, their first.

Yesterday we had snow and grey leaden skies which stopped the aircraft getting in. We placed the three main chimneys in place and packed them with glass wool. They were anchored by guys. We stopped work at midnight. Today, before leaving, I did some filming and also fixed the two thinner ventilator shafts in place. When it was complete the place looked like an Emett cartoon with the chimneys and chimney-pot hats held up by numerous rakish guy wires.

CHAPTER XIV

A Home by the Sea

For want of a better name we called it 'winter', though the winter and all other changes of an Antarctic year had little in common with the seasons of growth in the rest of the world. Cold and light was the Antarctic summer, colder and dark the winter. There was a kind of autumn, too, in which the sun set earlier each day until it disappeared altogether for the four months of darkness. And this Antarctic autumn was the answer to a colour photographer's prayer, with orange suns jerking and sizzling through strange mirages, golden snow beneath clouds of every conceivable colour—and the moon always in view, switching on like a lighthouse when dusk fell.

A photographer's dream, but one that was rapidly translated into a waking nightmare of frozen fingers and a sluggish shutter mechanism when you got down to the practical matters of filming. At Shackleton one day I had been helping Gordon Haslop and Ralph Lenton to build the roof of the workshop. The sun broke through a low sea fog, the recently-fallen snow sparkled, and long blue shadows ran from every building: the lighting was too dramatic to waste, so I gathered my cameras. Bunny and David Stratton were roofing the dog tunnels with old packing cases and canvas. I set up my movie camera to shoot the figures silhouetted by the sun, while around them the drifting snow was lit up brightly and gave just the right suggestion of cold.

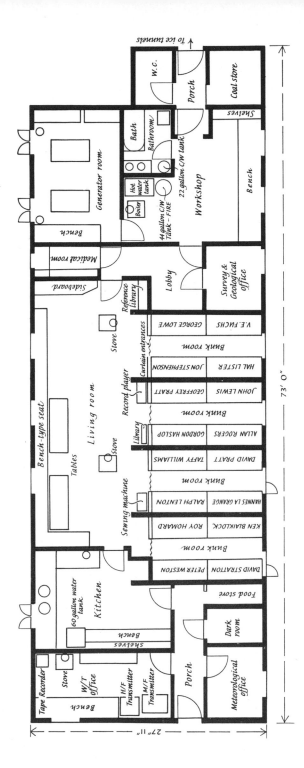

SHACKLETON BASE HUT PLAN

The two figures were hunched with backs into the wind and heads pulled into their shoulders. Bunny began to give me a running commentary on what he was doing and why.

A halo appeared around the sun and the framework of the workshop lay with bare ribs glistening like a desert skeleton. It was perfect picture material.

I carried my tripod cameras across and made some shots of the building work. A few seconds later the cameras froze.

Inside the hut at Shackleton the heavy, undressed cross-beams gave the impression that we lived under the roof of an ancient chapel. It was so solidly built—and although it will be buried now, and may float away as part of an iceberg, it will probably not be crushed, and I can imagine the seals sheltering in it when it becomes a floating polar summerhouse.

At one end of our home were four rooms: radio room, meteorological office, darkroom, and kitchen. The radio room was the warmest in the hut; it backed on the kitchen and contained a small stove, though its most efficient heating seemed to be the actual transmitter, a not very powerful set of only 350 watts, but able to carry our voices ten thousand miles to England.

This circuit was arranged to connect with any telephone in the British Isles, and we could make calls to our friends at a special rate of ten shillings and sixpence a minute. I never ceased to marvel when I heard the phone bell buzzing in a friend's house in England, and heard the operator say, 'I have a call for you from the Antarctic.' There was usually a pause for incredulity and often people even put the receiver down refusing to believe it was true. Reception was not always good, but great excitement was caused by this personal link which became the talking point of our week. Excitement, and also embarrassment, for most of us suffered at one time or another from the inability to express ourselves across the ten thousand miles with anything more inspired than 'Hello, dear, how are you, dear? I'm fine, how is everybody at home, dear?'

One day, when planning a call to England, I determined to rid my costly six minutes of these affectionate but fatuous bits of small talk, and sat down beforehand to prepare a batch of notes on the subjects I wanted to discuss.

When the call came through I cut the usual pleasantries as short as possible, then launched into the main topics I had carefully prepared. The atmospherics were a shade disturbing, but I went ahead until the voice from England interrupted with a remark I could not quite catch.

'What did you say?' I asked.

The comment was repeated but the crackling across the air made it yet again incomprehensible.

'What was that?' I asked.

'Never mind, it doesn't matter,' came the reply.

'Yes, but what *did* you say?' I persisted.

'I said . . . (more crackling, and the remark was lost) . . . but it really doesn't matter—don't worry.'

Not for several days afterwards was I able to detect the inaudible words. At Shackleton we were in the habit of plugging in our tape recorder for the phone calls so that messages could be played back. I listened several times to the recording of my dubious discussion and at last understood the elusive comment. Never again did I prepare a note for my long-distance telephone calls.

The remark was: '*You sound like a public lecture.*'

Our hut was divided down the centre with heavy pillars; the main living-room ended at the middle line and in the other half of the building were sixteen bunks separated into groups of four by low partitions; there were no private rooms and no doors on the bunk cubicles.

Bunny and I occupied one set of four (we each used the bunk space of two people when the original occupants went to winter at South Ice). This allowed Bunny an office or desk on which to write, and allowed me to spread my chattels. In addition to this extra bunk space I had my darkroom, which was small but extremely well equipped for the work I had to do. There were tables, sinks, shelves, enlarger and drying cabinet, and once the darkroom was established I added a record player and a small selection of classical recordings. In this way the darkroom became a haven which could be enjoyed at any time, for Bunny's antipathy to music meant that the record player in the main room of the hut could be used only on Saturday night and Sunday. Bunny regarded it all as a distracting din and the convention was soon established that musical silence was, if not golden, the easiest way of avoiding unnecessary strain.

In the large main room we lived a clublike existence. At one end of the living-room were tables and chairs; at the other a high bench which was a shelf for drinks; a dartboard; two maps, one of South Africa, one of New Zealand; a sewing machine; and collapsible canvas chairs. Around the walls in three separate units was our superb library of over a thousand books, including an almost complete collection of works on the Antarctic.

Electric power was rationed. We had a small generator and the radio transmitter took nearly half the output. Whenever I wanted lighting for filming indoors I had to arrange this when the radio was not in use. The transmitter was less efficient than it might have been (it was quite a problem to 'earth' the electrics when living on a floating ice shelf), and one could light a neon bulb merely by placing it upon any metal object in the room.

The warmth of the radio room had a further unexpected advantage; it was used by Ralph Lenton to grow mustard and cress; he tended this gay little allotment with great enthusiasm and we ate mustard and cress sandwiches every ten days.

Hannes la Grange lived like a brown bear in his small meteorological office. Wind gauges whirled and clicked and there was a constant hum of electrical devices. Charts lay in neat piles and the record books were in English and Afrikaans.

Hannes was devoted to meteorology and the policies of the South African Government. During the first year he had many arguments over the interpretation of *apartheid* and the racial problems of South Africa, but during the second year this had been 'talked out' and was seldom mentioned. No agreement could be reached in these arguments, which became acrimonious and heated: but we all agreed that Hannes was steadfast and honest to his purpose. It was not easy, as an Afrikaner, to take his place in our community, but Hannes was an undoubted success. He spoke English with a lilting tone, like a Welshman.

Fifty miles from Shackleton an American base had been established, and the radio operators made regular radio contact. One day it was arranged that Hannes should talk with the American meteorologist. Hannes gripped the microphone and said, 'My name is Hannes la Grange.' He continued slowly. 'I will say that again and spell it for you . . . Hannes la Grange. *H-a-n-n-e-s*, I say Hannes; *l-a*, as in French *la* . . . and now a new word . . . *G-r-a-n-g-e*, Grange. I say again: Hannes la Grange.'

The American listened and came back after a second's pause. 'Well, hello there, Hank—it sure is good to hear you.'

By the middle of May the sun was rising slowly just above the northern horizon where it remained for an hour or two and then disappeared. The mirages made icebergs float upside down in the sky. The blue sea turned grey as the 'young' ice formed more firmly each day.

Soon there was no morning sun to greet us at all. The long lull before the long continental crossing that would start in November had begun.

I was interested to discover that eternal night was on the whole far less monotonous than eternal day. Continuous daylight with all its blazing whiteness had many disadvantages, not the least of them the difficulty of ensuring a good 'night's' sleep of seven or eight hours while the sun goes on shining. But in

155

the dark we could work and live with a greater sense of community and relaxation. We could light up the darkness and switch off when sleep was needed. The moon's ghostly light was never a glare; the stars moved and wheeled all day; the aureola waved like a curtain, pulsating with changing colours with reds, greens and whites predominating. Our otherwise bleak Antarctic night was oddly satisfying.

The diversions, whether they were mundane and routine, or dramatic and unexpected, were always important in our winter lives. The most disturbing night of all was without question the night Geoffrey Pratt 'disappeared'. Ralph Lenton was on kitchen duties that week, and he had cooked us a succulent meal which may or may not have contained some heavy ingredient to provoke the dreams that afflicted nearly all of us during the small hours. At all events Ralph himself complained of a nightmare in which someone pressed hard on his chest attempting to cut off his air supply, and Bunny and I, normally sound sleepers, were similarly troubled.

At three o'clock in the morning we were awakened by a loud crash. I sat up startled and heard Bunny calling from the next cubicle.

'What the hell was that?' he snapped.

'I dunno, but I'm getting up to look,' I said.

We both jumped up, walked through the hut where the others were already stirring, and found Ralph Lenton investigating in the kitchen. With all of us the main fear was fire, but by the time a half-dozen men were fully awake we had satisfied ourselves that no fire threatened the hut. There was only one strange factor present: Geoffrey Pratt, who slept like a log most nights, was not in his bed. The blankets were turned back, he was not to be found in the lavatory, nor anywhere in the hut. Outside the temperature was at least −40°F.

We peered around into the freezing night and there was no sign of Geoffrey. Some distance away, however, stood the snow pit where he kept his instruments and gauges, and the only explanation of his absence was that he had gone there to examine the equipment. True, there was no earthly reason why he should do so at this unearthly hour, but there it was . . . Geoff was surely down at the pit and we all returned to bed muttering that if he were crazy enough to venture outside at 3 a.m., that was his affair.

Next morning I climbed out of bed and went for breakfast. Geoffrey was already at the table. 'Where the hell did you get to last night?' I inquired.

'Me? I didn't go anywhere, except in my dreams,' said Geoffrey.

'You went out at three o'clock or thereabouts,' said Bunny.

'What are you raving about?' asked Geoffrey. 'I never stirred from my bed.'

We told him the story of the alarm. But Geoffrey knew nothing about the night's events, and was adamant that he had not for a moment left his cubicle.

It was not long before he began shuddering ironically at the thought of his narrow escape. Geoffrey Pratt had clearly sleep-walked, heaven knows how far outside the hut—and by a miracle of fortune had taken the trouble to dress himself when he clambered unconscious out of bed.

If he had not done that, he would have walked to certain death in the outside air.

Bath night during the winter at Shackleton was an operation of some magnitude. It happened for each man only once every thirteen days and was a rare, pleasurable luxury. For some odd reason known only to the Crown Agents we were supplied with a bath that had no plug-hole. We had to cut the hole ourselves, and it was a major effort to drill through the heavy steel bath so that the water could drain away; when it did, a great pit was melted in the ice below.

My own method for getting maximum benefit out of the fortnightly event was not universally practised. During the day I had collected enough water (we melted the ice, of course) and after heating up the bathroom with a Primus stove, and boiling the water for the bath itself, I managed to achieve a near-Turkish bath atmosphere.

Steaming profusely, I scrubbed myself clean. Then, while still dripping wet with my whole body hot from the bathroom temperature of around eighty degrees, I walked naked straight out of the hut door into the ice tunnel where the cold was usually minus thirty or forty degrees.

The sudden attack from the cold night air, tolerated for only a minute or so, tingled and toned up the skin with the effect of a Swedish bath. From the sub-zero temperature I then returned to the bathroom and again soaked myself in the hot water.

It was always advisable to guard against practical jokers during this sortie into the cold, for the favourite sport of at least two of the party was to slam the hut door on any unfortunate naked man luckless enough to be caught, as it were, with his pants off.

Sixteen men—and no trained chef. Yet the standards of cooking turned out to be remarkably high, and especially so within the limited range of our rations. For many of us the duties of chef were a recurrent trial bringing a real anxiety. Lacking at first the good cook's basic enthusiasm, not to mention skill, we had to call on all our reserves of concentration in order to make a palatable success of the job.

We became a fiercely houseproud family, some more than others, and the kitchen was usually spotless—never more so than when Gordon Haslop was in charge.

Gordon and Ralph Lenton were the undisputed masters of the kitchen. Gordon was irate if anyone dared to serve food straight out of the pots and pans, for he always dished up our meals in casseroles, laid the tables neatly, and would forcefully declare: 'I'm not having you fellows eating like pigs when I'm on duty.' It was an unexpected facet of a personality who was known to be a relaxed and easy-going 'lover of a good time'.

John Lewis and the adaptable Ralph Lenton were also superb cooks, if anything better than Gordon, and for our midwinter Shackleton parties it was Ralph who created the spread of cheese straws, iced cakes and cherry-topped morsels with all the finishing touches that made the vital difference between his own and the commonplace results achieved by others. Ralph good-naturedly guarded a jarful of glacé cherries which he kept under his bed.

Although I belonged to the mediocre class of chefs, along with those who disliked the cooking and kitchen chores, I became—like them—reasonably adept at all kinds of dishes I would never have believed myself capable of producing. At teatime, for example, the man who took his turn in the kitchen soon found he could not get away with a few sweet biscuits— we had to learn to make Swiss rolls, bath buns, sponge cakes with tasty fillings, and a host of housewifely frills beyond the plain cook's usual fare.

It was extraordinary, too, to catch oneself out in momentary feelings of disappointment when the men for whom you slaved all day over the proverbial hot stove showed something less than the hoped-for measure of appreciation. Like some tearful young wife with a boorish husband, many of us confessed to a faint touch of outraged chagrin if the party came in to dinner, sat down to a good hot meal, and then in silence consumed the proudly-presented result of the effort, chewing automatically while reading a book.

Reading at every meal, however, was soon an accepted custom. I think it was Bunny himself who started it, and eventually it was agreed to maintain a 'quiet' table for those who wanted to pore over books, and a 'noisy' table for those preferring to chatter. There was a suggestion of method in Bunny's encouragement of the reading habit, for there was no doubt that he disapproved of any discussion touching on the expedition's plans or progress. Indeed, the one spark that could be guaranteed to jerk Bunny away from his book was the start

159

of a conversation, even a desultory chat, on some expedition topic such as vehicles and equipment.

One day a group of three or four were listening with interest while Geoff Pratt held forth on the subject of the gloves we wore. 'These things are no bloody good,' said Geoffrey. 'I wouldn't mind betting I could design a far more efficient glove for conditions like ours.'

Bunny glanced up sharply from his book, took off his glasses, laid them on the open pages, and spoke. 'When you know a good deal more about Antarctic conditions,' he said quietly, 'you'll also know more about gloves. These gloves have been designed after years of experience—and I think you'll find they'll do the job they were intended for.'

Bunny replaced his glasses, picked up the book and went on reading. After his intervention the glove topic, like many another, was dropped.

A different sidelight on the subject of our hands was by this time being revealed whenever we had certain jobs to perform outside the hut. The skin on our hands and fingers was gradually adapting to the cold. Hands became thicker, tougher, very much drier, and we found it possible to handle metal parts and similar cold objects at temperatures well below thirty degrees of frost. Along with this facility, however, came a painful disadvantage familiar to most housewives. Badly split fingers, with deep cracks at the ends, were to be a discomfort for many months to come. Finger nails were also affected; in the cold they ceased to grow, broke off short and remained brittle.

Sore hands were possibly the cause of a camera accident and a highly-skilled repair operation carried out by our doctor, Allan Rogers. Returning from one of my frequent filming expeditions around the site, I dropped my Rolleiflex camera on the hut floor, seriously jamming the shutter release knob and damaging the interior. Luckily, Allan was a master technician who could carry out the minutest repairs to the most delicate parts. This time he stripped the entire shutter mechanism and restored it perfectly.

As a doctor he was kept decidedly short of employment. We had little sickness, no serious illnesses or fractures and certainly no troubles involving operations. As a dentist, however, he was exceptionally busy. The Antarctic cold had a disastrous effect on our teeth, causing fillings to drop out by the score.

Also a physiologist, Allan carried out an interesting experiment to study the 'horse-power' rating of a human being. This involved measuring the quantity of food each man consumed and the amount of energy he put out. In the cause of the study we all wore the mask and breathing machine with which he recorded our intake and output of oxygen.

The week of our midwinter came in the third quarter of June. As if to remind us that darkness would now progressively lessen, the sky showed a delicate red sun-glow to the north. There was a quickening of energy in almost everybody, an involuntary surge of enthusiasm for what would be called spring—and the approach of the day when bursting activity would be needed to prepare for the long crossing which was, after all, the *raison d'être* of our work and waiting through the four months of winter at Shackleton.

Meantime, all signs of bursting activity were being harnessed for a less solemn purpose: the Shackleton hut party to celebrate Midwinter Day. We also held parties whenever anyone had a birthday to celebrate, but the midwinter round of festivity was undoubtedly the biggest bender the Antarctic had ever known.

It began before noon with a cocktail party at which our new vehicle workshop, known as the Chapel, was ceremoniously declared open. This was greatly enlivened by the efforts of Gordon Haslop who staged a twelve-minute fireworks display.

At three o'clock we sat down to a vast midwinter meal of roast turkey, potatoes (these had been frozen under the ice ever since *Magga Dan* departed), with plum pudding, sherry, champagne, coffee, cigars and liqueurs. Afterwards the whole party slumped quietly into sleep, unable to touch an extensive buffet prepared by Ralph Lenton and John Lewis. But by evening the party spirit had returned with gale force and continued throughout the next day and night. In the midst of it all we did not forget to send messages of goodwill to all the other expeditions, at the Pole, and elsewhere in Antarctica, and especially to the men of our own group who were doubtless indulging themselves in like manner on Hillary's side of the continent.

Ralph Lenton's skiffle band, with double-bass manufactured from a tea chest, a broom handle, and twine, filled the night with noise and a kind of music that was not half as bad as it might have been.

The drink flowed freely (there would be no more liquor once we started the crossing). The music blared on. Ralph performed a dance of seven veils, garbed in red drill marker flags taken from the petrol dump on the ice. Everyone watched him and cheered. Only Geoff Pratt was unmoved—seated with his back to the orgy, his eyes and brain unbelievably concentrated on some fascinating dissertation in the *Encyclopædia Britannica*.

The dance reeled to a crazy conclusion. Misty-eyed as we were, most of us were aware that with midwinter gone, our days of gracious living were strictly numbered.

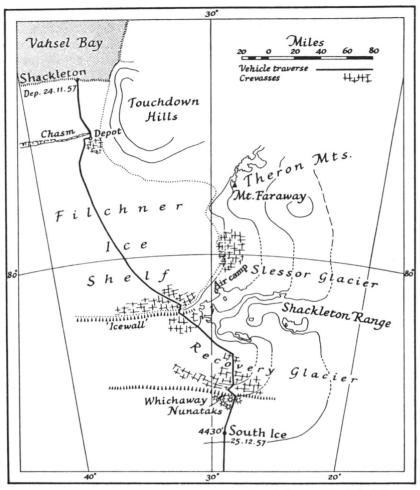

Shackleton to South Ice

CHAPTER XV

Twelve Miles a Day

For exactly one hour on a Tuesday morning towards the end of August, the sun made its first diffident appearance since May. It was only a fraction of the orb that showed above the horizon, looking at us quizzically, but it *was* the sun, a bright golden blaze and the finest sight we had seen in four months. That day the temperature was −28°F, and there was a 30-knot wind hurling drift and spumes of snow.

But despite the lengthening days, the glimpse of spring sunshine was something of a false promise. September roared in like a lion. For the first two days of the month we had a temperature of −60° F. and gale winds of up to 54 knots, which means 63 miles per hour. And with our little foothold at Shackleton attacked by high drift as never before, all effective work came to a halt.

Bunny's original plan, reckoning on weather conditions a good deal better than we eventually experienced, was to send into action the first of five field parties by the first of September. On that day, as Bunny reported in his official account, *The Crossing of Antarctica*, six men and four vehicles were to leave to 'investigate the structure of the great chasm south of Shackleton. . . .

'On the 10th,' he continued, 'we planned to relieve South Ice by air, and on the 13th two men and one dog team were

164

to be flown to the Theron Mountains for survey and geological work. On the 27th four men, with two dog teams, were to fly to the western end of the Shackleton Range, where they would be set down on the ice shelf close to the mountains. Their first task would be to find and mark a route from the heavily crevassed ice shelf up the steep and broken "ice wall"; this done, they would make a survey of the mountains. On the 30th, four men and four vehicles would leave on the all-important reconnaissance journey to South Ice. By the 22nd October it was intended to have everyone back at Shackleton preparing for the start of the trans-continental journey on the 14th November.'

But these plans, as Bunny aptly added, had to be 'greatly modified'.

As things turned out, the 'chasm' journey was abandoned; blizzards wrecked the flying programmes; the relief of the South Ice men (Ken Blaiklock, Hal Lister and Jon Stephenson) was delayed for several weeks; and not until the 8th October, more than a week behind schedule, was it possible for the four vehicles of Bunny's all-important South Ice reconnaissance to set out from Shackleton. Thus far, the route to South Ice was known only from the air; no land crossing had yet been accomplished.

Instead of reaching South Ice on the 22nd, however, Bunny and his three companions arrived on the 13th November (only one day ahead of our original scheduled departure date for the main crossing of the continent), after a hazardous trip of thirty-seven days during which they suffered the total loss of one vehicle and the temporary abandonment of another.

While they were gone, we at Shackleton grew daily more despondent on several counts. Bunny's absent team included not only his own deputy, David Stratton, but also both engineers, David Pratt and Roy Homard. Several of our vehicles still lay buried in the drift, unproved, untried on the terrain we had soon to face; and as the days wore on we became ever more conscious of the almost total lack of training and vehicle preparation for the field of operations. In addition, some of the party at this stage had not even the experience of tenting on the ice for so much as a single night.

The time factor nagged us constantly. From the far side of the continent Ed Hillary and the New Zealand support party were already setting out—after a vigorous spell of pre-journey exercises, dog training, and modifications to their vehicles—while we sat cooling our heels at Shackleton.

Bunny's rate of progress during his South Ice reconnaissance had turned out to be no more than ten miles a day, which was precisely half the planned daily average of twenty miles regarded as a minimum for our main journey. And although it was soon crystal clear that we had no hope of setting out from Shackleton by 14th November, we were frequently embarrassed into evasive responses when we were plagued by the Press, the BBC, and even our own London headquarters, demanding to know our departure date. *Proceeding according to plan*, the stock formula for reply over our Shackleton radio, had a depressing ring in our own ears if not for those of the outside world. It was not surprising that despondency was rife at Shackleton by the time our leader returned from the South Ice reconnaissance.

Bunny and his team flew in with John Lewis at ten o'clock on the evening of the 15th November. The next day he called one of his rare round-table conferences, gave us a detailed picture of the problems along the difficult route to South Ice, discussed the recasting of our plans—and announced with an unmistakable insistence that we would now leave Shackleton, regardless of our state of preparedness, on 24th November. For this definite decision we were all thankful.

Vehicles and fuel apart, we had done everything possible to ensure the readiness of equipment and supplies. The checking of rations alone provided Ralph, Ken, John Lewis and me with several days' work. The food boxes had come out from England two years earlier in *Theron*, and we could not take any risk of assuming that all was in good order, so we went carefully through every food crate, examining every carton, tapping every tin.

The final rush, lasting eight days, was a time when sleep was limited to the bare essential necessary for working efficiency.

The food, and the dogs' food; the sledges and the clothing; the seismic apparatus and the explosives; the radio equipment and the camera equipment; tools, ropes, skis, tents, cooking utensils and Primus stoves, first aid supplies . . . with the deployment of all these and much more it seemed we would never have time to finish. Yet above all these stood the twin anxieties —*fuel and vehicles, fuel and vehicles,* thundering repeatedly through our minds like train wheels.

How many miles to the gallon? We did not know. On Bunny's South Ice recce it was a little more than a mile for a Sno-Cat and two for a Weasel, in both cases less than we bargained for. And what did we need in the way of spares? On the recce they found that fan belts and radiators wore out at a rapid rate. And would we get through with enough anti-freeze? That too was being eaten up at an alarming speed.

Every day of travel across the continent would mean burning a weight of fuel almost as great as the load of our entire supply of food for the whole crossing. Eight vehicles consuming two hundred pounds of fuel every half-hour. . . .

On the shoulders of David Pratt and Roy Homard the worries of fuel and vehicles would fall. By the morning of the 24th David was tossing spares into sacks and boxes, racing against the clock and refusing even to stop for food.

It was a Sunday. Zero hour was fixed for half past two in the afternoon. Tension was affecting everybody on the base; we had worked well into the night and no one got to bed much before 5 a.m.

Shortly before lunch Bunny climbed into his Sno-Cat *Rock 'n Roll,* which he would share with David Stratton, drove out on the ice about two hundred yards, and planted the vehicle with its nose pointing south. I then drove my Weasel *Wrack and Ruin* over to the spot and pulled in behind the leader. Inside the Weasel I had fixed a variety of racks and slings to hold the cameras, and pasted sacking over numerous holes to keep out the snow. For a while I would have no sledge to tow behind me; mine was lying eight miles ahead, dumped by the earlier reconnaissance party, fully loaded with two and a half tons of fuel.

John Lewis and the RAF boys were seeing us off. Fortunately they noted how badly things were going and bestirred themselves to prepare the last meal we would consume at Shackleton Base. All except David had a stand-up farewell luncheon; still rushing to meet zero hour, David went without.

It was already past two-thirty. Bunny looked at his watch and spoke impatiently. 'For heaven's sake let's be gone by three o'clock,' he said.

But three o'clock arrived and still we were not ready to move. Someone had forgotten to check the steel wire tow ropes which were the safety lines for our sledges, and the last-minute discovery meant that all these had to be bolted together. Bunny was furious, for this caused hours of delay. He and I completed the bolting.

We were almost beginning to wonder if we would get away before the next morning when Bunny in no uncertain terms put an end to any further shilly-shallying.

'Listen, everybody,' he said. 'I'm getting out of Shackleton tonight—even if it means camping only half a bloody mile away.'

The challenge was fair enough. At a quarter to seven we moved off.

Three Sno-Cats . . . Bunny and David occupied *Rock 'n Roll* at the front of the column; David Pratt and Ken Blaiklock were in *Able*. Roy Homard and Ralph Lenton drove *County of Kent*.

Two Weasels . . . *Wrack and Ruin* contained me and my cameras. Allan Rogers, the doctor, drove *Rumble*.

One red-painted Muskeg tractor . . . manned by Jon Stephenson who with Ken Blaiklock would soon take over the dogs (already awaiting us at the South Ice depot) and become the first men to drive dog teams to the South Pole since Amundsen did so in 1911.

The evening was cold, grey and windy, and a strange metamorphosis took place as soon as we were on the move. Tensions fell away, faces relaxed and smiled. I raced *Wrack and Ruin* at a good twelve miles an hour up and down the line, filming and firing each 'still' camera in turn.

The convoy was going smoothly along the first few miles of the nine hundred that separated us from the Pole. Irritations and delays forgotten, our comradeship was visibly strengthened.

As the motors roared and the Cats, Weasels and Muskeg rolled forward in line, I stood on the roof of *Wrack and Ruin* working the cameras in an effort to record the great exodus from Shackleton; but the weather had clamped down, there was no blue sky, no sea to be seen in the background—just the vehicles trailing past at three or four miles an hour with their drivers making rude signs at the camera. Photographically it was all rather flat, but more than ever now I was glad to be a member of this expedition. Jumping off the Weasel to the ground, I placed the tripod and cameras inside, swung myself through the door into the bucket seat, and hurried after the cavalcade.

My snow goggles began to steam up and the ice in my beard dripped in the warmth as I tracked in close to David Pratt's Sno-Cat. With hands off the steering tillers I rewound the movie camera and fired a long burst at his whirling tracks. David grinned and thumbed his nose. I pulled away, lining the yellow Cat and the red Muskeg in the camera sight and fired another long burst. This is tremendous fun, I thought, as I sped to the front of the column, fired all the cameras again, and then, satisfied for the moment, pulled out to the side and bowled along southwards with the party.

The first day was wholly enjoyable, especially as I had the freedom of filming from an unladen vehicle, the luxury of a Weasel to myself with the cameras slung from my home-made canvas bags, and a roving commission. The fretting, the muttering, the sick feelings of excitement, the nerves, that had sometimes made me a pain in the neck to Bunny in the days before departure, fell away easily. I had always been critical of the lack of cohesion, of bad communications, of being kept in the dark about expedition plans, of the failure to give both men and vehicles at least a taste of rehearsal before the big journey began; and I tended also to be the channel through whom Bunny would receive the grievances of others in the party. As I followed the yellow tail of Bunny's Cat into the wilderness I felt a little contrite and resolved to be more reasonable.

Jerking *Wrack and Ruin* out of the tracks, I overtook the leading Cat. Bunny sat seriously at the wheel in steel-rimmed snow glasses and black leather helmet. His eyes looked steadily ahead judging the surface and turning occasionally to the compass mounted just above his gaze. As I overtook him he glanced across to me, grinned and paternally waved me out of his way.

Beside him, David Stratton poked a black horn out of the window and blew a loud blast at me. Immediately it set off a succession of bells and hooters and raucous whoops from the following company.

Every man was glad to be on the way.

The first night we made only seventeen miles before camping shortly before midnight; but the break was now complete— Shackleton lay behind us and the frenzy of the departure faded. My Weasel was now fully occupied hauling the almost crippling load of petrol drums we picked up along the route.

Wrack and Ruin was the oldest vehicle in the convoy. There had been no time for an engine overhaul, but it ran sweetly, started without trouble and had brand new tracks and sprockets; so her heart and undercarriage were good even if her appearance was dilapidated, and it was certainly that; the scaly paint on the cab was blotched with pieces of canvas and sacking, glued with a rubberized concoction over the many holes; the doors hung awry, secured with pieces of wire and always tending to fly open when *Wrack and Ruin* was in motion; the glass in the windscreen was cracked and held together with sticking plaster; the windscreen wiper worked fairly well but in heavy drift it gave up and I drove with my head round the door. Although I cursed her and many a time wished fervently that she would break down so that I could drive a comfortable Sno-Cat, she never did.

On the second day out the cloud was thicker and lower, the wind more searching. Driving was easy as long as there was somebody making tracks out in front. At first I wondered why David Stratton moved so slowly. But leading was very different from following. In the grey whiteness nothing stood out clearly; the hillocks and hollows were indistinguishable from the smooth; and the direction could be maintained only by steering on the compass, a task demanding relaxed concentration.

In second gear we played follow the leader at walking pace. Several weary miles flipped by on the dashboard counter, and my attempts at photography were unrewarding in the shadowless grey. I fell to wondering how much extra fuel we burned in low gear travel; we were swallowing anyway roughly forty gallons every dozen miles.

Far away, beyond practical thought, lay the Pole. Between it and us was a blank of days and miles which had no shape, no reality or measurement in my mind. Nine hundred miles to the bottom of the world, to a magical point that stood nine thousand feet above sea-level. Nine hundred miles without roads, across a desert of ice; over mountains; up and on across a waste land uplifted high. It frightened and enthralled me.

Of the first three hundred miles I had long ago caught a bird's-eye view, having flown over it many times. It was spread in my mind like a piece of the modern 'feelie' geography that lays a continent in three dimensions on a table, a neat scale model on a board. From Shackleton stretched an undulating ice shelf, an immense floating carpet covering a hundred miles of sea. After the first forty miles a rhythmic pattern of gentle hollows and crests ended abruptly where a huge chasm yawned. The gash was several hundred yards wide, a couple of hundred feet deep, and many miles long; seen from the air it had conjured up somebody's operation, a clean open cut across a white belly. Still unexplained, the chasm may be a hinge or fracture point where the tidal action is slowly breaking up the ice shelf, which will eventually float into the Weddell Sea as a vast iceberg, taking Shackleton Base with it.

Beyond the chasm lay one hundred and sixty miles of smooth snow carpet leading to the point where the Antarctic continent really begins to lift itself out of the sea, rising abruptly, bursting through the thick ice cover with a black mountain range, the Shackletons, that stood squarely across our path.

Towards the chasm and the mountain barrier we drove on. . . .

Damn the leader! Why must he stop so suddenly without a signal? But in a moment I knew something odd was happening with Bunny and David Stratton up front. As I climbed out of my cab David Pratt was already running forward towards *Rock 'n Roll* and I ran after him. 'Here's trouble—big trouble,' groaned David as soon as we reached the spot.

Rock 'n Roll had burst the lid of a deep crevasse fifteen feet wide. The front of the Cat was bent forward and downwards; they would have plunged right in if the pontoons had not buried themselves in the far wall and the roped sledges in tow held back the rear. Below the dangling Cat gaped a black hungry hole, with loose snow trickling away to fall soundlessly into the cavernous depths. Bunny, magnificently calm, leaned out of the cab, peered into the death-trap and said: 'I don't think this is a particularly good side to get out.' Bunny and David climbed from *Rock 'n Roll,* and sprang across a gap to safety.

At first sight the recovery looked impossible, with the Cat straddled across the chasm like a crippled elephant caught in a trap. Everybody walked around kicking and prodding. David Pratt minutely examined and tested the ground disbelievingly. Before long someone made a facetious comment that eased the strain, and then the tide of ideas began to flow and a workable plan emerged. I ran to my Weasel, unstrapped the skis and tripod, snatched three cameras and skied back to film and photograph the scene; my side of it was easy.

During the weeks to come we were to experience a score of these crevasse incidents. Anything from five to twenty hours of preparation were needed before the actual shifting of the trapped vehicle could begin; but when this stage was reached the vehicle was hauled to safety in as many seconds.

All five vehicles were used to pull Bunny's *Rock 'n Roll* out of the crevasse. Five drivers fixed their eyes on a controller who conducted them with the utmost precision in a movement of pull and counter-pull. When the operation began, steel wire ropes were tied to the front and rear end of the Sno-Cat. Then three other vehicles had somehow to get around and across the crevasse in order to pull the victim forward. On such occasions the rescue machines were either in tandem or lined up three abreast, attached by the wire ropes to the vehicle caught in the crevasse. If we merely pulled at the vehicle, however, its back would certainly fall into some yet more perilous position—so to avoid this a counter rope was anchored at the rear, generally with two Weasels to hold it, putting as much tension as possible on the trapped machine. Sometimes we pulled them out from the front, sometimes backwards, according to how they lay in the crevasse.

After the intoxication of the first day, our second was somewhat sobering . . . with only twenty-five miles accomplished and the near loss of a Sno-Cat. What the others were saying in their tents I did not know, but alone in mine I swallowed my pemmican (that archaic Polar standby made of dried meat and fat), wrote up my film log and lay back to ruminate once again on the journey ahead. If we ran into too many crevasses like this one, which still gaped near us, we would not get far. Dogs might after all be the best form of transport for the journey. . . .

The idle reflections ended suddenly when I heard the Otter roaring low over the camp. It circled and came in on a long cautious approach to land. I knew this caution of old—it *must* be Gordon Haslop.

It was Gordon, who touched down and taxied in beside us. He burst open the door, put out his head and shouted: 'What have you been doing to our ice shelf—it looks very untidy from the air!' But the wisecrack was swept aside by Hal Lister, who jumped from the aircraft with his sleeping-bag, doffed his woollen hat and continued the Mad Hatter's talk by adding: 'Hello! hello! hello! Isn't it all enormous fun?'

Hal, who was to be my tent companion for the rest of the journey, had flown from South Ice to make our party ten. Gordon departed for Shackleton and we settled down for what was left of our sleeping time.

Early next morning I was awakened by more of Hal's incorrigible forced jollity. 'Will you have brown toast or white, sir?' he said, pouring thin porridge into my aluminium plate. I sat up, still in my sleeping-bag, rubbed the sleep from my eyes and without enthusiasm took the steaming plate. Hal was at it again . . . 'Don't take more than you can eat—saving waste will help the Fleet!' He subsided gracefully after I threatened to pour the porridge down his trousers.

Hal had a vast store of naval and sea-going stories which he related with such perfection that I could never decide if the incidents truly happened. He was a man who left school in his early teens to join the merchant navy, roamed the world as a young seaman, and when war was declared in 1939 he joined the Royal Navy to serve in destroyers; although he had spent years at sea I noticed he still suffered, like me, the miseries of sea-sickness. He had read the works and frequently expounded the theories of Marx, Trotsky, Beveridge, Social Credit, Rousseau, Keir Hardie and others; at political meetings he liked to heckle, without regard for party or platform—he just enjoyed the heckling, he said. Honest and inquiring in all his science (he was a lecturer at Durham University), his main work as our glaciologist consisted of studying the micro-meteorology of the six feet immediately above the surface.

Before leaving Shackleton Bunny had posted on the notice-board a list of our six tenting pairs with a footnote stressing that these were final and there would be no swapping during the journey. At first I thought this was a mistake but looking back I realized Bunny was right. Over the long journey where the going was mostly a monotonous unchanging ice desert, with occasional moments of fear and excitement, there had to be an attitude of hardness and an intelligent determination to quash the inevitable personal differences and be ever aware that we simply must live cheerfully together. The philosophy took the general line, 'You volunteered, so get on with it.'

We rolled forward towards the 50-mile depot (established the previous year by Ken Blaiklock), and then Bunny's Sno-Cat stopped again. This time the engine was overheating. David Pratt hurled out the seats and floor mats, lifted the bonnet and sniffed like a terrier.

'It's a coolant leak,' he said. 'Somebody get a can to save the drips.'

David fretted and searched until he found where the heated battery box was leaking the precious cooling fluid. It took an hour to replace the part, and our total delay was nearly five hours; this was but the first of many similar hold-ups.

The idle hours spent standing about, although unavoidable, made us cold and fretful. Jon Stephenson sat on his engine bonnet, engrossed in the *Confessions* of Jean-Jacques Rousseau; the rest of us just sat around showing no initiative.

When we did move we were breaking through crevasses after driving forward only a few hundred yards. Here, abreast of the great chasm forty miles from Shackleton, lay a crevasse belt five to seven miles wide. On foot, which meant on skis, we would first have to probe and work slowly through.

This probing of crevasses for the vehicles to cross in safety was a long and exhausting business. By working for twelve to fourteen hours each day we managed to cover only two miles, or maybe two and a half. Working in pairs over a stretch we forced metal rods, five feet in length, down into the snow. Many crevasses were covered by a lid of winter snow three to five feet thick; the holes below could not be detected from the surface and would easily allow a man to pass on foot, or even a dog team and sledge, without a tremor; but they could not and did not allow the passage of six heavy vehicles pounding them with thirty-five tons in all. With no warning the snow lids just broke away.

Whenever a crevasse was found by probing, an inspection hole was first made in the lid. Sometimes we dropped down into them on the end of a rope, but mostly we peered from the surface to see the width of the supporting walls. If the gap were more than three feet we peered along underground to where the crevasse narrowed (usually thirty or forty feet from the widest part), and there we probed again and marked the narrowest gaps with flags. In the most difficult areas, with interlocked crevasses, we found delicate routes which necessitated driving the vehicles through the marker flags and judging the pathway to the nearest inch in order to ensure a safe crossing.

Day after day we pounded the way ahead of the vehicles, our long poles probing suspiciously. Choice of a companion was haphazard and varied, giving individuals a chance to exchange views in a way that was not generally possible on the

176

David Stratton

Bunny Fuchs

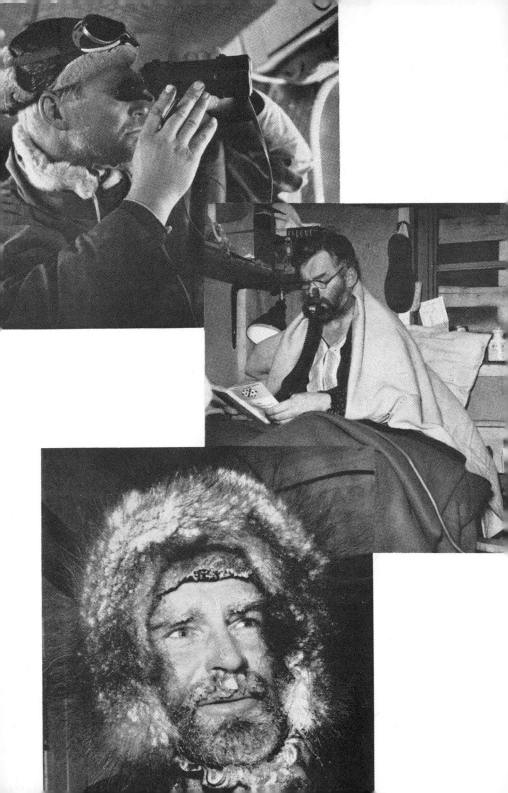

David Pratt

Sno-Cat in the first crevasse—twenty-five miles from Shackleton

The Polar Plateau
Above : Jon Stephenson's team the day before reaching the Pole, and
below : Sno-Cats at 10,000 feet after leaving the Pole

The Skelton Glacier
Above: Hal Lister breaking camp in high wind, and *below:* Two Sno-Cats,
a mile apart, hurrying down the Glacier

Ed Hillary and myself on arrival at Scott Base at the end of the expedition

journey. Sometimes I walked with David Stratton, and once we had an odd discussion on the public schools of England. I was keen to hear his views as an old Harrovian on what he thought the school had given him, and to know if his considerable self-assurance—a pleasantly well-bred superiority—came from his schooling; but it was difficult for David to be anything but flippant about this. 'My tour of the vineyards of France was the best education I ever got. . . . Move over your way, there's a bloody big hole just here.'

David, who was a hard worker, seemed to have been born to lead. His godfather was the veteran Lord Mountevans (the late Evans of the 'Broke', who also captained Scott's ship) and he grew up with Antarctica in his veins. 'Ever since I was five years old,' said David with his slightly tired accent, 'I have been patted on the head and told, "You will go to the Antarctic".'

The first crevasse area took us four days to cross. It was perhaps the most uncomplicated belt that we had to deal with, but at the time it shook our optimism considerably. Bunny's first party to South Ice had tried to convey to us the tedium, care and frustration of testing the route yard by yard, and now that we were all faced with the same experience we began to realize the significance of Bunny's determined belief that his 37-day reconnaissance was the crux of the expedition's problem.

At the end of our four days of punishing progress many of us were dispirited, for nine miles in four days was not going to get us rapidly to South Ice, let alone the Pole. But Bunny was unshaken even when we heard by radio that Hillary had reached Depot 480, his second depot on the Polar plateau, 480 miles from Scott Base. We had done forty miles!

And then, suddenly, dejection changed to high spirits when fortune began favouring us again in the early days of December. In a couple of sparkling, windless days we shook free of the unsafe area near the chasm to set off in a line like ships at sea, tossing, rolling, throwing sprays of snow from the vehicle tracks like a bow wave.

We made forty-three miles one day and sixty-five on another. During this fine spurt we were to pick up fuel dumped during the reconnaissance journey to South Ice. Leading as usual, Bunny and David were undeniably proud of their navigation, and as we completed the mileage to their estimated position of the dump we all searched the white wastes about us. No dump could be seen.

Bunny checked his mileage and direction and said: 'I can't understand it—we're right on the spot now.'

We drove forward another mile and stopped. David Pratt then caught sight of the depot—several miles to our right. We streamed away, each making our course to the dump, thinking up droll remarks to make about Bunny's navigation. But Bunny intrigued us all with a sample of his old unshakable confidence, saying without the flicker of a smile: 'I can't understand it—the depot must have shifted!'

Sixty-five miles in thirteen hours was good travelling, and one of the best distances of the whole crossing; not until we reached the Ross ice shelf within a day or two of Scott Base did we accomplish anything similar.

I never ceased being impressed by the sight of the Sno-Cats ploughing forward in line like cruisers going into battle, with flags and pennants flying and always the flurry of snow spraying their tracks. Each rowdy engine bellowed with a shattering note as the 230-h.p. motor ate fuel at the rate of one mile to one gallon of petrol. Every hour our monsters used enough fuel to take my small English saloon car sixteen hundred miles.

What a difference, too, between this mechanized Antarctic travel and the days of Scott manhauling his sledges, or Amundsen swishing quietly along with dog teams. Our method was warmer, with long boring periods spent sitting at the wheel while the motors roared; it was also infinitely dirtier, with all the grease and petrol fumes.

By the 4th December we were nearing the end of the great

ice shelf that stretches over the sea, and we came in sight of the Shackleton range and the junction between the land ice and the sea. This was the properly-named 'ice wall'. Before we could reach it, however, we had to cross a badly crevassed area covering eleven miles.

The ground looked deceptively solid. Crevasses in the Antarctic I found very different from those in the mountains of New Zealand or the Himalayas. Here there was no change on the surface, no buckling or pressure appeared to twist the ice —but the crevasses were there, all the same, covered by the winter snow.

As the vehicles set off towards the ice wall I waited behind with a telephoto lens which magnified the distant mountains into something more impressive. Against this superb background the Sno-Cats moved like yellow beetles, or perhaps hunch-backed mechanical creatures running on a moonscape. I could see the shot as the opening to my film. Reloading the camera, I hurried after the van which was now two miles away.

While I rattled along in the tracks of the others I was disturbed to see small crevasses, cracks of nine inches to a foot wide. I increased speed to seven miles an hour and hurried over them. Behind *Wrack and Ruin* the heavy sledge slipped across without sinking. Soon I caught the tail of the party and passed them to pull in behind David Pratt. The field began to straggle as more small crevasses were opened up. The leading Cat, with Bunny and David Stratton, rumbled on towards the flag that marked the first dangerous crevasses, their sledges opening wider and wider holes.

Before long the inevitable happened. *Rock 'n Roll* broke through and sank her tail into an enormous cavern. I drove up and parked within a few yards. Miraculously she was jammed across the top of the hole, but the faces of the engineers were very pessimistic when they saw that the heavy steering rockers under the chassis were snapped, and heavy bars bent.

179

The recovery procedure was used as before, and in bleak, windy weather *Rock 'n Roll* was once again hauled to the surface. The job of repairs lasted two days.

Then came a week more of probing on foot, with painful progress—a whole week, and eleven miles. The days were now hot and windless, quite unlike anything I had ever expected. We worked and sweated in shirt-sleeves, some even stripped to the waist; the endless prodding made arms and backs ache.

Looking along the line of prodders reminded me of the pilgrim track to Badrinath, where the devout crawl and measure their length, with all manner of uncomfortable antics, to acquire 'merit' as they go to Vishnu's shrine. Here, stripped to the waist in a world of snow, each man with his staff would move a step forward, thrust the staff into the snow, force it down to the hilt until he was bent double, with his ears and muscles tensed to listen and feel . . . then up with a jerk and another weary step. I hoped we were acquiring merit, too.

Along the firmer stretches I was sure the crevasses were not too bad and said we'd be chicken-hearted if we did not drive boldly over this ground. Twenty yards later the pole would push through to nothingness underneath and I hurriedly changed my attitude about being chicken-hearted. Here, we devout pilgrims also changed our ritual, for looking along the line one could see only a row of backsides in the air with heads on the ground as if praying to Mecca; they were of course peering into the depth of the crevasse.

When crevasses had to be crossed the order of running was changed. Sno-Cats were the more valuable vehicles and we wished to protect them, so our two Weasels would lead the slow convoy; and in all the miles of crevasses we crossed (and sometimes fell into) Bunny still drove the leading vehicle. His was undoubtedly the most dangerous and nerve-racking position, never shared, and it was a remarkable performance requiring an iron will.

It usually took a whole morning to probe and flag a crevasse mile; it was always with relief that we stopped the backbreaking monotonous task, to stand exchanging views on the most dangerous areas while eating a spartan lunch of two dry biscuits held apart with a half-inch of butter and a layer of Marmite, washed down with two cups of cocoa from a Thermos flask. Motors were meanwhile started and warmed up to working temperature; crash helmets were donned, the drivers stepped in fastening their safety harnesses; Bunny gave a signal and simultaneously we moved forward, changing gear and watching the heavy rope that linked us. It had to be just right—not so loose that it dragged and was overrun by the tracks, not so tight that it dragged the leader and broke his pace, judgment and steering. The leading Weasel had to set the pace and steer to within inches of the marker flags. If he sank into a crevasse he needed just enough slack rope to accelerate smoothly forward if he thought he could race across the gap.

A steady, well-paced, fearless progress was Bunny's technique, and he was superb, with not a hint of shying or faltering before a nasty jump. Although sometimes frightened, I drove behind him feeling the most intense pleasure at this game of skill. First in line was the most dangerous position, last in line the next; and second to the leader (where I usually drove) was probably the safest.

After seven tormented days we shook ourselves free of the long crevasse run and moved up, then over, the ice wall. Off the flat ice shelf, climbing up and up, to run along the glacier a mile or so from the black peaks of the Shackletons.

Crossing the Recovery Glacier (so named simply because of the difficult vehicle recoveries involved) occupied a full week. We drove at right angles to the glacier's downward flow—fifty miles from bank to bank—and the first stage was astonishingly easy. It had taken four and a half days during Bunny's October reconnaissance, and he was jubilant, as we all were, when the fine warm weather helped us to flag a route through in a single day.

So delighted was Bunny at this uneventful crossing that he declared a half-holiday, which we used to change the engine oil and grease, tighten tracks, and draw breath for the next encounter with broken ground. We enjoyed the break and Ralph painted a sign advertising his café in the stern of *County of Kent*, where tea or hot soup was brewed.

Not for the first time I was finding that whenever I filmed an exciting action, I did not see it in much detail. First thoughts went always to the camera, to the job of moving it slowly, smoothly, keeping the action in place; and seen through the squinting blinkers of a viewfinder the impact of the circumstances is dulled. Insensitive to detail, except for the detail of the image in view, it is then that dangers become blurred.

While crossing the Recovery Glacier we were halted by lack of visibility, and I was foolhardy enough to suggest to David Pratt a camera angle from the ground. He agreed to drive the Sno-Cat over me if I lay between the line of his oncoming tracks. So, with the camera tucked into my face, I went down on my back in the snow. I had crawled under a Sno-Cat often enough to grease the tracks—but at speed the twelve inches of clearance around a prostrate body seemed terrifyingly little. David made his run and as the tracks flashed past I pressed the button and got my shot: but once was enough.

The glorious Indian summer which had warmed us in the first half of December ended abruptly when low clouds hurried in from the north, heavy with moisture from the sea. This brought 'whiteout', the atmospheric Antarctic version of a pea-soup fog, and we drove forward eighteen miles bumping and pounding an iron-hard surface, straining our eyes to see.

We now aimed to position ourselves in line with mountains which bounded the southern bank of the glacier. Just as we camped to take food and sleep, a slight improvement in visibility showed us to be three miles away from our intended course. Snow fell gently but insistently and continued to fall as we moved three miles westward to enter the troubled ice of the southern bank.

A day later we moved thirteen hard miles in the grey snowy weather. Four of the party skied ahead and we crept forward roped together. By the end of the day's run the black rock faces of the Whichaway Nunataks were only four miles away.

Next morning the nerve-racking battle with crevasses was on again. Ken Blaiklock and David Stratton skied ahead to flag a line through a forest of ice towers and shapeless hummocks that were often twenty feet high. Now we were crossing the last of the Recovery Glacier where the flow buckled and twisted past the nunataks. Of all the miles of crevasses this was the most difficult and the most dramatic. From the sky we must have looked like ants toiling through the white debris of a meringue.

And so it went on. Twice in one day Ken Blaiklock had narrow escapes in crevasses. With men and machines the near misses were becoming distressingly common. We longed to cross to the safe solid ice slope we could see beyond, so near and yet so far.

Bunny still drove the leading Weasel and there was stress in his face as we prepared to drive over the last two sections. An air of resignation had crept in—our luck could not hold out indefinitely. Bunny lit his pipe, grinned and slipped into his harness. 'Okay, let's go. I'm sure it will be all right,' he said.

We moved forward, with blue cracks and sagging snow on all sides under the towers of ice; up and over domes and hillocks; down slopes heaving on the brake levers; around ledges, over crevasse after crevasse; eyes on the rope and flags. There was not a moment to think of anything but driving. We came out of a gully, turned and jumped three hard-lipped crevasses and drove up a slope between the nunataks.

We were through without a casualty.

We did not then know it, but this was the last of the crevasses for many weeks; there was to be no further trouble until long after the Pole when descending the other side of the continent.

South Ice lay forty miles ahead and we drove there in a couple of days.

It was all over except for the back-slapping and expressions of relief.

'Oh, well driven that man,' said Jon in his most cultured Australian. 'Marvellous,' said Hal, laughing, 'less than two thousand miles to go.'

I dashed ahead to film the arrival.

In just under one month—twenty-nine days, in fact—we had covered nearly 350 miles. The Pole was still 555 miles distant, and the far side of the continent sprawled for another 1,250 miles beyond.

CHAPTER XVI

Pole Cats

OUR third Christmas dinner in the Antarctic was eaten under distinctly bizarre conditions at South Ice depot a few hours before we set off on the journey to the Pole. The hut we had erected the year before was now buried by the winter snow up to the last extension of its chimneys, and sixteen feet underground there were ten of us congregated for dinner and the Queen's broadcast. There was not much room for ten thickly-clothed men in the little hut designed to house only three.

Hannes la Grange, who flew to South Ice several weeks earlier, and Geoffrey Pratt who stayed on after the reconnaissance journey, had welcomed us to the depot and were now rejoining us for the drive across the continent.

We were staying at South Ice for three days, to dig out the petrol which lay buried there, and to overhaul the vehicles. And we were leaving with the biggest load of the journey, for it would not be possible to refuel until we reached the depot that lay 550 miles past the Pole on the route to Scott Base. This was Depot 700 (seven hundred miles *from* Scott Base) and was already established according to plan by Hillary and his party.

Crammed into the South Ice hut, we were all set for departure, a relaxed and happy band of bearded brothers, with grease blotching our wind-proof clothing and newly-sewn patches over rents and holes. Greasy leather gloves hung from

185

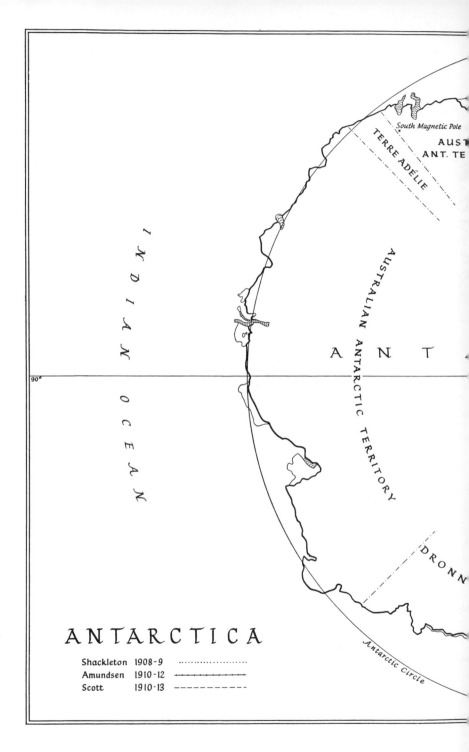

South Magnetic Pole

TERRE ADÉLIE

AUST
ANT. TE

I N D I A N

AUSTRALIAN ANTARCTIC TERRITORY

A   N   T

90°

O C E A N

DRONN

ANTARCTICA

Shackleton	1908-9	·················
Amundsen	1910-12	+++++++++
Scott	1910-13	---------

Antarctic Circle

everybody's neck harness; faces glowed in the warmth of the hut; our bellies were full after three days of feasting on tinned vegetables, fresh lamb and steak which had been frozen for the year awaiting just this moment.

Bunny raised his voice and I knew this was the departure call. 'I want to get away from here in half an hour. Is everybody ready? David, what's the final count on fuel . . . ?'

I opened the heavy door, stepped into the long corridor of ice and went to the pool of light that shone down the entrance shaft. In a blue alcove cut in the ice I grabbed my precious box marked 'Film' and climbed the steep ladder. Reaching the surface I looked out on the vast plain of dazzling ice and the great dome of sky where wisps of cirrus cloud hung at forty thousand feet and more. Everyone else was still below ground and our yellow and red vehicles stood in line dressed like flagships on review day. Every possible rag of bunting and bits of crêpe paper fluttered from radio masts. I set up my camera and tripod within a few feet of the fading wind-sock; this, the latticed instrument tower and four chimney pots were all that marked the featureless surface.

South Ice was now 'To Let' . . . before long it would be totally buried . . . and perhaps it will be found again a hundred years hence, or a thousand, a quaint historical oddity, a trace of evidence that we were there.

Our exodus had a brave romantic touch about it: Christmas Day, with flags flying, streaming off in close array, leaving a six-inch furrow across the ice. The sky was blue and the horizon, though featureless, was not without promise.

For a few hundred yards we ran west and then, turning along a line of stakes which had been aligned most precisely, the compass was checked and we headed south along the 29th meridian.

Five miles later we came on a small tower built of snowblocks and bearing a cardboard notice. *Only 550 miles to go. Next stop the Pole*, it said. Ken Blaiklock and Jon Stephenson, driving the two dog teams, had left two days ahead of us to mark the route with snow cairns, do some survey work and flag any dangerous crevassed areas.

From South Ice we began a new routine. Science was our goddess and each of the party began to worship at his own pet shrine, each writing his testament of revelations. To Geoffrey Pratt's goddess was given the most time and importance; using seismic methods he was measuring the thickness of the ice layer over the continent. His Sno-Cat *Haywire* pulled a mixed cargo of petrol, food and explosives; and inside his Cat £12,000-worth of electronics measured the time taken for the explosives to send shock waves down through the ice and bounce back from the rock below. Hannes la Grange, travelling and tenting with Geoff, had his meteorological gadgets mounted in an old food box secured on the outside of their Sno-Cat.

We had crossed the mountains and now at 5,000 feet we rose steadily in gentle waves to a shimmering horizon day after day. Like camels, the vehicles drank from their humps and made their grumbling, temperamental way across the desolate miles. It was a strange emasculated place on which we made not the slightest impression, and I could never come to any understanding with the cold impersonality of this land. Even the hottest deserts have their softer moments, a miracle of rain, an oasis of growth, a fossilized sign of some nomadic traveller; but there was nothing more impersonal, nowhere more un-yielding and monotonous than this white continent—growth-less, heatless, rainless, timeless. As Jon Stephenson put it when I lounged in his tent drinking tea and talking of such solemn matters: 'Yer dead right, I am glad I came, *but* . . .!'

A few days after leaving South Ice we overtook Ken and Jon with their two lightly-laden dog teams. The dogs were running well, tails held high, covering a regular twenty miles each day regardless of the surface roughness.

For Ken, who had spent five years in the Antarctic, driving a dog team to the Pole was a dream being fulfilled. Amundsen was his hero and now he was the first (and possibly the last) to repeat this dog marathon. Taking another light load of food for the dogs and themselves, they disappeared whooping and howling over the horizon.

With *our* ponderous inanimate train we drew into a tight circle and spent a day welding broken bars on sledges. A new though not unexpected handicap was slowing our progress— sastrugi. Sastrugi describes the surface when the wind packs the snow into hard ridges; at the same time many loose ice particles, also blown by wind, carve the ridges into shapes not unlike a choppy sea—a sea, if one can imagine it, that is frozen into immobility. Our solid hickory sledges were shod with plastic runners connected by iron bars shaped like a capital A, and extra cross-pieces were added to the framework before leaving Shackleton. The devilish sastrugi proved to be higher, wider, harder and far more destructive to tracks and sledges than we had tried to allow for, so here we were, a few days after setting out, heating, straightening and welding the broken bars. These troubles alleviated, we moved on.

A few days later and for no apparent reason, sudden violent attacks of vomiting and diarrhœa began, first in one tent and then another. The cause baffled Allan Rogers, who first suspected the Thermos flask of incubating bugs in the sugar when we left it lying overnight as we sometimes did. Great care was then taken but still various people were affected for a day or more.

About two hundred miles from the Pole our altitude was somewhere near 8,000 feet, and we were driving well strung out through endless fields of sastrugi. The two dog teams ran easily over the ploughed ice, one ahead and one behind me, while nearly a mile ahead the leading Cat was forcing implacably onward.

As the weeks of driving passed I had grown almost buckled into the uncomfortable sitting position in the Weasel where my feet were pressed forward on the steel floorboard. Inactivity had left me ill-prepared for the shock that was coming. Ahead I saw Ken's dog team running slowly with their driver riding on the sledge: this was wrong—the driver should ski to one side, calling encouragement to the dogs.

The sledge stopped and the dogs began to mill about, tumbling over one another, fighting. Of Ken there was no sign, so I hurried forward.

Reaching the sledge I jumped out, leaving my engine running. Then I saw a revolting sight. Ken lay helpless in a paroxysm of vomiting while the dogs fought and struggled to eat it. Grasping Ken's ski I leapt in shouting, kicking and swinging, to get the yelping dogs away from him. Ken recovered slightly, got up and swayed, his face ashen, walked to the Weasel and crawled in to lie shivering across the engine cover.

Five minutes later I got him settled inside a sleeping-bag among the spanners, grease guns and gaskets of Roy Homard's Sno-Cat. Ralph Lenton took over my Weasel, and I found myself in command of the panting dog team. The dogs were now greatly excited by these events and a change of drivers seemed to bring out new energies. I released the brake, shouted the command to go—and they went. I had just enough warning of their excitement to hold on to the sledge as it careered forward, bucking and twisting over the hummocks. Soon I was gasping for breath. There is no command for 'Go slower' in the husky language, only 'Go' and 'Stop'. The command for 'Stop' is a long-drawn-out 'aah'—and I found it could not be shouted when you were running and panting at an unaccustomed altitude. I feared for the sledge as it smacked up and over to become airborne where the hollows opened beneath. The dogs had their tails high and I cursed them.

After a few hundred yards the sledge jumped a bank, twisted in the air, landed on its side and slowed quickly to a stop. I lay down on it to regain my breath, then strode to the head of the line of dogs and addressed them. They sat blinking as I pleaded for less frivolity. I heaved the sledge upright and the mad rush

191

began all over again; eventually they tired, and as the miles increased we settled into a long steady lope which I could manage.

Next day I drove again, and we covered thirty miles. My muscles ached, and my throat was dry and sore from gasping in the cold air; lips got cracked by the wind; my clothes were soaked in sweat; when we camped that night Hal Lister cooked the pemmican and cocoa and I quickly fell asleep.

On the third day the sastrugi was less troublesome and I rode much of the twenty-five miles on skis. Even though a cold wind made me turn my head away from the blast I enjoyed the run, which was my last day of dog driving. The real disadvantage of these runs was that my nose was very susceptible to frost-bite, the skin on the end dying and flaking away. Ken recovered and took his dog team on to the Pole.

At latitude 89°S the dense ridges of sastrugi had given way to a gentler surface of softer, smoother snow. Our southerly course was still uphill; every day we gained more altitude. At 9,000 feet the horse-power produced by our motors was less than half their sea-level performance. The Sno-Cats, their fuel consumption now giving less than a mile to the gallon, still hauled their loads easily and could have moved faster, but they held back for the dogs, and also for me driving *Wrack and Ruin*. My Weasel load had been reduced considerably—I was now pulling about one ton of petrol—but even so I maintained only three and a half miles an hour in second gear with my foot hard down. For days now I had been running the motor at maximum power every foot of the way; and I poured oil into the engine more often than petrol. Exhaust fumes caused me a good deal of worry and headache.

Then I contrived a better if queer-looking method of progression. I arranged the Weasel cab so that I could stand upright with my feet on the seat and my head out of the trapdoor in the roof. With two pieces of light rope I controlled the steering tillers and also tied the throttle—wide open. In this way I drove non-stop for hours on end playing hare and tortoise with the faster Sno-Cats. Standing in this position I could also film passers-by.

And I could read; this was my absorbing pleasure as I rolled forward in the tracks of the vehicle ahead. As the miles slipped by I read *War and Peace*. The volume I had was a remarkable one which I handled with sentimental care. Turning the thin rice paper pages I would come unexpectedly on a pressed primula or a brown tea-stain, for this copy had spent five years in the knapsacks of travellers in strange lands. I first saw the book on Everest, wrapped in a plastic bag with an unused shaving kit, where Michael Westmacott loaned it to John Hunt to read. Next year I saw it again with Charles Evans, who carried and read it when we explored the flower-strewn valleys east of Everest. Charles packed it with his paint-box when he led the expedition which climbed Kangchenjunga. There he passed it on to George Band who read it under the precipices of the Yalung face.

George Band handed it to me for my trans-Antarctic journey. Today it still has the flowers and tea-stains—and now also a lingering aroma of pemmican. I keep it still—unmoved by all the taunts about my sentimentality.

Often as not I ate my frugal lunch while we were on the move. Lunch consisted of four coarse-oat biscuits covered with butter more than half an inch thick (the polar ration allows nearly half a pound every day). To this could be added sardines which I thawed out on the engine cover for an hour before eating. Sardines were a rare delicacy, and I had secreted a few tins in my tool kit at South Ice. Everybody had some kind of titbit. Bunny's passion was sweet jam, and he seemed to have a store which he and David enjoyed to the Pole. Geoff Pratt had the best part of thirty pounds of honey stuffed in tins identical with the explosive cans. Hal and I had access to this hoard, which was marked 'Seismic spares', and I livened up morning porridge with a spoonful of honey.

Hal would come over to my Weasel on days when we stopped for lunch, and we sat discussing my progress with *War and Peace*. 'Well, where have you got to today?' he would ask as he climbed aboard. We called such pauses for biscuits and butter our Literary Luncheons. For light relief we would sometimes turn to the Royal Geographical Society's *Hints to Travellers*. It contained a mass of good sense and serious information on polar matters, yet with the flick of a page one could jump from hints on the price to pay an Eskimo for a husky to advice about camels ('No camel can be properly ridden in boots') ; or about a cure for blistered feet ('It is a good plan to soap the inside of the stockings before setting out. A raw egg broken into a boot, before putting it on, greatly softens the leather') or on emetics ('Drink a charge of gunpowder in a tumbler full of warm water; if not gunpowder, soap-suds—and tickle the throat').

As for the general range of conversational topics among members of the expedition, it was intriguing to see how the balance shifted as the crossing of the continent progressed. In fact, the pattern was a repetition of experience on Everest, where Griffith Pugh (a physiologist we were later to meet at the Pole) made a diverting survey of the 'percentage rating' of different subjects discussed at different stages of the climb.

During the early days on Everest he found that three main topics, apart from the journey, took up a good deal of conversation time. Politics and world affairs; food; and sex (i.e. women) were the big trio.

At the beginning, sex was at the top of the list. World affairs came second. Food absorbed only about ten per cent of the talk.

By the time we were approaching the ice-fall and the Western Cwm, the order of priority had fundamentally changed. Food was the paramount subject, having soared to something like fifty per cent. Politics was an also-ran. Sex had dropped completely from the climbers' interests.

194

On the 3rd and 4th of January messages were exchanged between Bunny and Ed which were to have world-wide reverberations. Ed, concerned about our slow progress, had advised Bunny to leave the vehicles and fly out from the Pole station to wait another year before crossing the continent; Bunny had firmly rejected this advice and saw no reason to change his plans. On the morning of the 6th he called a meeting to put us in the picture (the word went around in one of our more impudent and disrespectful whispers, 'Matron wants to see you all before school begins'). He read out the two messages, Hillary's and his own. Cabling his alarm about the serious delay in our plans, Ed had declared that by leaving the Pole in late January we would be heading into increasing bad weather, and that his mechanics, regarding such a late journey as an unjustifiable risk, were not prepared to wait and travel with our party. Agreeing with this view, Ed pointed out that we still had a major journey to reach the Pole, and suggested flying out to Scott Base with American aircraft; 'return to civilization for the winter and then fly back to the Pole station next November and complete your journey.' He added, 'If you decide to continue on from the Pole I'll join you at Depot 700. Sorry to strike such a sombre note, but it would be unfortunate if the sterling work you've put into making your route through to South Ice and the Pole should all be wasted by the party foundering somewhere on the 1,250 miles to Scott Base. I will go ahead with the stocking of Depot 700, and I will leave at the Pole station full details plus maps of the route from Scott to the Pole.'

Bunny's reply said he appreciated Ed's concern—'but there can be no question of abandoning journey at this stage.' He went on to say that our vehicles could operate at minus sixty degrees, that he did not expect such temperatures by March, and that we would wend our way, 'using the traverse you leave at the Pole.'

After reading the messages Bunny told us again that there

195

was no question of our not continuing the journey. 'I know we're late,' he said, 'but after all, Scott didn't reach the Pole till the 18th January, and we have got vehicles. We're going to arrive about the same time, and then we shall have the benefit of Ed's proved route out.'

There was no discussion of either the messages or the decision —and we drove on. Nobody in the party had the slightest wish to postpone our crossing of the continent; on that score we were in full accord with our leader.

On 7th January we learned, almost by accident over the radio from the BBC in London, the news of startling developments in our affairs. Ed had apparently sent a confidential message to the Committee of Management in London and by an unfortunate blunder in Wellington, a copy of this was given to the Press of the world who were now moulding it into a headline storm of controversy, although its scale we did not fully realize, or could scarcely have believed, until we reached the South Pole.

By the twenty-fifth day of the journey from South Ice we had completed exactly five hundred miles. With only fifty-five miles to run, the Pole was at last within striking distance. But there was no quickening of the pace, no undue excitement, for it was regarded by Bunny as a foregone conclusion, a mere expedition interlude before the second and longer half of the journey. This, at any rate, was the viewpoint he always emphasized.

I remembered this day, the 18th January, not so much because it was the eve of our arrival at the Pole: it was the day I finished *War and Peace*. The surface of our route had smoothed, and after a solitary lunch I settled down to the last pages while *Wrack and Ruin* pitched very gently across the shallow depressions. I sat reading with my head out of the roof under a blue sky with the temperature around twenty below zero. I left Tolstoy's hero in a state of ineffable peace, and swamped by the impact of the novel I drummed forward still lost in situations that were a century behind the times.

196

My sleep that night was light and fitful. When we got going in the morning there were ripples of exuberance showing on the surface; even Bunny displayed something by calling for all flags. I straightened my flagstaff; the small New Zealand ensign had faded in the wind and sun—the Union flag in the corner was distinguishable but all trace of blue had gone from the four stars of the Southern Cross.

The Pole was still hours of sitting and several pints of oil away from us. A few thoughts of Everest flickered in my mind and I knew that the climax of this expedition was not the same. The Pole was not the end of the expedition: we were still not half-way across the continent. Yet although the Pole was flat and only a man-made point, it still held a powerful attraction. I thought of my companions, and of our leader. Bunny was an extraordinary man. When we were up in the air with excitement he gently depressed it; when we were down he ignored it, pretending depression was not there. What drove *him*? I never saw him give the usual signs of emotion when some vital point in the journey was within grasp, and by the time I was full of excitement at approaching the Pole, he had accepted the coming fact, put it beyond him and was planning his moves ahead. Certainly a desire for knowledge drove him, but if the visionary dreams of adventuring were also a factor, then he had learned to hide them.

After a long day's run and the usual chores we settled down for sleep. Our position was 89° 30′S, about thirty miles from the Pole. On the morrow we expected to reach the American base built on the plateau at 90°S. I had almost drifted into sleep when I heard a distant droning of engines. The noise grew louder and I stuck my head out of the tent to find two American Neptunes flying low over the camp. They circled several times, and Ralph ran to the radio to speak with the pilots, who said they had on board Ed Hillary and Admiral Dufek, the commander of American Polar operations. They would be landing at the Pole to await our arrival.

197

Next day we drove forward with our navigators calculating the precise distance left to run. 'According to me,' said David Stratton, 'we should have about eleven miles to go and we'll probably be a couple of miles off to starboard.' His reckoning was 'spot on'. From a crest we searched the horizon and Bunny and David simultaneously saw the dark smudge. Shading my eyes against the sun I could perceive the outline of a tower and a dome to the left.

The South Pole at last.

We turned left, to seek a line of flags placed to mark the way in. Our pace was funereal, my Weasel could only make a mile and a half an hour and the dogs were very, very tired.

The midnight hour passed and the sun blazed down from a cloudless sky. We moved into close order, with every flag flying. Bunny and David led in *Rock 'n Roll*, followed closely by me in *Wrack and Ruin*. I was determined to keep up and film as much of the arrival as I could.

Half a mile from the huts and towers a self-conscious group awaited us. As Bunny's Sno-Cat stopped, the figures burst into life and began milling around. I had jumped out, festooned with cameras to record the moment when Bunny met Ed Hillary—the magical moment when the two sides of the expedition joined hands across the continent—but all I could see was a heaving mass of people.

It was an excited meeting: the Pole does not receive a lot of visitors and we had not seen a new face for months. I filmed and photographed wherever I could. Then, doffing my hat and extending my hand to Ed, I made the shamefully obvious remark, 'Sir Edmund Hillary, I presume.'

The four stark rectangular structures of the Pole Station had now been camouflaged, banks of snow rounding the angular squares, moulding the base into the Antarctic scheme of things. On a wooden platform stood a black sphere from which radiosonde balloons were released. An orange-coloured box surmounted by two clear plastic domes was where vigil was kept on the auroral activity. A thicket of masts was laced together by aerials.

Parking my overheated Weasel between the Sno-Cats, I stepped out stiffly, put the engine covers on and swaggered into the station. Friendly American voices said 'Hi there' and 'Howdy' and 'Glad to see you' and went quietly about their business. I could tell they were holding back just a little; they were thoughtful hosts and knew instinctively that the phlegmatic Englishmen did not want superlatives—at least not yet. I walked into the mess hut, where thick warmth wrapped around me like a strait-jacket. The unaccustomed sensation made my arms and legs heavy and I realized how tired we had become when I saw my companions slumped on stools with drooping heads.

Our hosts gave us coffee. They wore neatly-pressed slacks, shoes and open shirts; some had luxuriant well-combed beards. Bunny's Boys, they called us, and we were an overdressed, motley crew, in torn and baggy windproofs, knives hanging from our belts. With scaly, cracked faces we must have looked like a bunch of elderly delinquents as we fingered the radiogram and caressed the steaming coffee pots.

The Americans had prepared an enormous eggs-and-bacon feast. They plied us with food, laughter, speeches and goodwill, but none of us could do justice to the food because our stomachs had shrunk.

'I've got a bag of mail for you,' said Ed Hillary later. He dumped the sack of letters at my feet and stretched out on a bed in the sleeping-hut. I tipped out my pile of correspondence, a whole year's accumulation weighing fourteen pounds; it included an OHMS envelope containing my income tax demand.

We began to talk of families, and of mountains; and then apropos of nothing Ed said: 'Well, the Press have certainly gone to town on this business.' He meant, of course, the frenzied

199

efforts of the correspondents and newspapers (the 'Race for the Pole', as they inevitably called it) who had been focusing attention on the two principal characters of our expedition. All the flamboyant headline ingredients were present: two parties converging on the polar plateau; two men leading overland journeys to the Pole; two radically different personalities.

It took a long time and much discussion to piece together the picture that I now believe to be the truth.

One thing I knew better than most people, from my experience of Hillary on our expeditions: there was no malice in Ed's character and actions. He does most things for the intrinsic joy of them—and getting to the Pole in three commonplace tractors, having finished his assignment with time to spare, was his method of brightening the bleak cold weeks of 'hanging about'.

Bunny had originally believed that we would arrive at the South Pole for Christmas. He told Hillary we would pass the Pole and reach Depot 700 about the same time as it would take Ed's party to establish the depot. Bunny assumed that because of his superior equipment—particularly his Sno-Cats—he would have an easier and faster journey than Hillary's team with their dogs and supporting aircraft—dogs to make the route and aircraft to ferry their supplies.

What happened on *our* side of the continent? We spent Christmas not at the Pole but at grim South Ice, several weeks behind schedule. What happened on Hillary's side? They completed their Depot 700 a fortnight earlier than anyone had dreamed was possible.

Resenting the distortions that crept into the telling of this story to the world, I became increasingly convinced that the context of our positions and timing was absurdly glossed over in the assessments of the so-called Hillary-Fuchs dispute.

When the New Zealand men had done their seven hundred miles from Scott Base as a *support* party, they learned that we on our side were still no more than three hundred miles forward as the main crossing party, with almost two thousand miles still to travel.

Ed told me: 'Quite simply, our feeling was that there was no point in waiting. We'd established the depot, we'd brought in the fuel and the food. What was the use of hanging around?'

Moreover, Ed and his party were living in tents. There was no hut at Depot 700. So the prospect of waiting several weeks on the polar plateau with nothing to do had no appeal for anyone. Rather than a long cold sojourn in the tents, his team favoured flying back to Scott Base.

But Hillary, who had decided to bring his tractors on to the plateau, had other ideas. He knew that towards the Pole, ahead of Depot 700, lay crevasses. And after persuading his party to remain, he radioed Bunny offering to clear these crevasse areas so that our path would be marked. Bunny replied: *Okay—go ahead.*

Shortly afterwards Ed sent another message. This time he told Bunny that unless we wanted yet another depot (a depot still nearer the Pole, beyond 700) he proposed paying a visit to the Pole station himself. His cheerful words were: *I'm going on a jaunt to the Pole.* Bunny replied that to ensure success he would like another depot a hundred miles beyond 700, but unfortunately radio conditions prevented the despatch of this message for forty-eight hours and Hillary, when he received it, stated that he had pushed on and had passed the point of no return. It was this brief radio communication failure which later forced Bunny to ask for additional fuel to be flown to Depot 700.

Ed reached the Pole station on the 4th January, when we were still nearly four hundred miles away from it, and acting, as he believed, with a sense of responsibility for the safety of our party (and knowing also, as we did not, what lay ahead of us), he had sent Bunny the notorious message advising him to postpone the full crossing. It was a private communication from one leader to the other, advising on the conditions of the

201

territory with which Hillary was familiar and on his calculations based on the short distances we were travelling each day.

The real blunder had been made in Wellington, where Hillary's message to the Committee of Management in London was handed to the Press. It seemed to me, when the shouting eventually died down, that both men had behaved in a logical as well as characteristic fashion.

The restless Ed Hillary, whose 'jaunt' to the Pole had no selfish, glory-seeking intentions—and who made our speedy exodus possible—just did not realize the potentials of our Sno-Cats in the last stages of the crossing. In different circumstances his counsel could have been right . . . it was proved wrong.

The enigmatic Bunny Fuchs, whose inner motives baffled us, had with dogged persistence got us across the bottom of the world as planned. He could have been wrong . . . he was proved right.

CHAPTER XVII

Hurry! Hurry! Hurry!

W E were on the way out and well past the Pole before my amazing *Wrack and Ruin* was finally abandoned in the loneliest part of the continent. The aged, tired Weasel was left to succumb to the death implicit in her nickname, and I joined one of the majestic Sno-Cats for the first time.

We had left the Pole station and the well-dressed Americans on the 24th January. One thing was certain: although there had been no dramatic 'race' between Fuchs and Hillary during the journeys *towards* the Pole, we were without any doubt engaged in a race against calendar and weather throughout the 1,250 miles of trekking *away* from the Pole. Bunny's prophecy that we would double our daily rate of progress was soon turned into solid fact as we went into the 'downhill' run averaging thirty-four miles a day.

Covering the gruelling 350 miles which had so often galled and delayed us between Shackleton and South Ice had taken four weeks. The next 555 miles from South Ice to the Pole had lasted a little less than four weeks.

Now we were aiming at 1,250 miles in a mere five weeks. To achieve it we were aided by Hillary's clear tracks leading like tramlines to Depot 700, and by the fact that we no longer needed the dog teams; the dogs were flown out from the Pole station by the Americans.

203

After leaving the Pole we climbed for almost another thousand feet to where the crest of the continent is well over 10,000 feet high. For sixty miles we ran at that altitude, and then began the shallow downward glide all the way to Scott Base.

Depot 700 was about the same distance from the Pole as South Ice, but we did the run at more than double the speed, with good surface and the advantage of the marks left by Ed's tractors. Etched in bas relief on the windblown surface, much of the track was still intact after more than five weeks.

By this time we were also spacing out our scientific work, making seismic shots every forty or fifty miles instead of our usual twenty.

The sense of urgency increased as we moved; we took less sleep, travelled harder than ever before in order to push up the daily mileage.

Ed Hillary, who flew in from Scott Base to join us for the last run out, shared a tent with Bunny for the rest of the journey.

The last weeks on the polar plateau were bitterly cold. All activities were more miserable to perform and there was bleakness in every mile. The tents were just that much colder now, and condensation from breath and cooking formed on the inner skin. Despite every possible piece of clothing the cold crept through from below; at −40°F I found that even the sheepskin mat and eiderdown coat under my double sleeping-bag were failing to keep out the chill. We usually lit the Primus a long time before breakfast was needed. Hal and I would then lie in torpor until he grew animated enough to start the day with his favourite cry: 'If my mother could see me now—she'd buy me out.'

With breakfast over and the seismic shot fired, the four Cats drove forward. There were now three or four people to each vehicle. In the lead were Bunny, Ed Hillary and David Stratton, and with them rode Hal, tucked away in the icy cabin. Roy Homard's Sno-Cat *County of Kent*, which had no partition

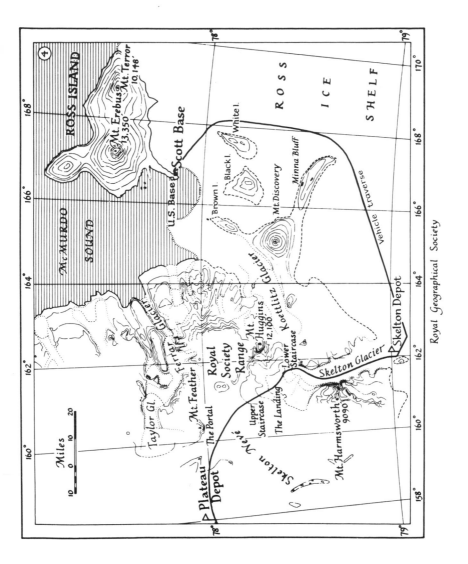

Royal Geographical Society

behind the driver, was more communal. He and Ralph Lenton shared the driving, and in the rear Ken Blaiklock and Jon Stephenson, relieved of the dogs, rode among the piles of spares, tool boxes and radio equipment. Ralph had rigged a Primus to boil water for soup and drinks.

With Geoff Pratt and Hannes I travelled the last nine hundred miles in Sno-Cat *Haywire*. We were the only Cat team working as a trio; each half-day we took one of three positions in strict rotation—driving and maintenance, co-driver making meteorological and navigational log reports, or lying in sleeping-bags at the rear.

Haywire was packed tightly with seismic recording apparatus, developing tanks, geophones, radio, Thermos flasks, delicate motors, cameras and film. Between these ranks of frozen impedimenta we laid our three sleeping-bags and wriggled into the top one when it was our turn to rest.

For some time the remarkable Sno-Cats had been showing signs of wear; we had considerable trouble with steering rods and a variety of mechanical breakdowns. But for me there was a peculiar new thrill in handling the big machine. It was highly disconcerting to take the Sno-Cat's wheel for the first time. The steering was so different from that of a car.

The steering wheel was turned in the same manner, and with about the same effort. But then for a long moment nothing happened, and I was panicked into turning even further, thinking the steering had broken away. Slowly, seconds after the first action, the huge Cat began to change course, leaning over into the corner, going round fast. I began to correct—but again nothing happened and again I panicked as we continued circling. Suddenly the turn began to unwind and the Cat lumbered forward in a straight line. It felt as if I had nothing to do with the whole process.

The reason for the delayed action lies in the four-wheel steering, operated by powerful hydraulic rams which twist the front and rear pontoons in opposite directions, and while this is happening the Cat continues on course before she rapidly comes around. After a while I mastered it; through the big steering wheel it was just possible to feel the pressure and tremble as the steel pontoons slid along with the clackity-clickity-clack of track rollers. The ground surface controlled our speed, which varied between two and ten miles an hour.

Compared with Hillary's tractors these were monsters that swept across the land with throaty bellows; their power and handling were like flying a modern aeroplane after learning on an ancient open-cockpit trainer.

We moved on—and on again, picking up food and fuel at each of Hillary's depots.

We dropped down a wonderful scenic route to the head of the Skelton glacier, descending between 15,000-foot mountains to sea-level in another couple of days.

We heard the news even as we pressed forward that the few remaining links with the past were breaking . . . old Admiral Skelton, who was at the Antarctic Club dinner I attended four years earlier, and Lord Mountevans, who was David Stratton's godfather, had died. Both were with Scott nearly fifty years ago.

Running out on the Ross ice shelf, we passed not far from the spot where Scott himself died.

We travelled fast in the last three days, over the ice shelf to Scott Base.

We arrived at three minutes to two on Sunday, the 2nd March 1958, after a trans-Antarctic journey lasting ninety-nine days, which was really ninety-eight days, as Bunny said, when you reckoned that we crossed the date-line on reaching the Pole.

Within the hour the message came through to say that Bunny had a knighthood.

*   *   *

The expedition was over . . . three years culminating in three months of battle across the buried continent, not so much be-cause we assumed it is there, but to discover with some scientific certainty *if* it is there.

And it is.

OF INTEREST TO PHOTOGRAPHERS

Few photographers, amateur or professional, are ever likely to take pictures in the cold ice deserts of the Antarctic continent. But I will list here the impedimenta that I took, and make some comment on the particular problems of expedition photography.

Three different records were being made simultaneously and I list these in the order of priority which I gave them:

(i) ciné filming (a film for general release),

(ii) black and white pictures (for newspapers, advertising, and Bunny Fuchs's official account of the expedition, *The Crossing of Antarctica*),

(iii) colour transparencies (for lectures and journals and the book).

Any photographer will know that handling three different cameras at once is difficult. I felt at the time that I was falling between stools and that the best I could hope to do was compromise. In filming and photographing an expedition on the move, the only realistic way is to shoot where and when one can, for progress cannot be interrupted: no one will stop anyway! I tried to anticipate events by being in position beforehand, but manipulating three cold cameras with two cold hands can be very frustrating.

Around my neck on leather straps hung two cameras: a Rolleiflex loaded with black and white and a Leica loaded with Kodachrome; in my hands, or hanging from a wrist strap, I carried a Bell & Howell ciné camera and, whenever practicable, a tripod. With three cameras comes the complication of three different settings for the lenses. I tried to overcome this by making each camera as near as was practical to a 'box camera' setting. On the ciné camera I taped the speed ring on twenty-four frames per second (sound speed), set the distance at twenty feet (which gave me a depth of focus from five feet to infinity), and hardly ever moved the aperture from $f.$10 in open sunshine. On the Rolleiflex I set the shutter at 1/25th of a second, the aperture at f.16 and focused approximately for each shot and fired rapidly. For the Leica the shutter was hardly ever varied from 1/100th of a second with an aperture of $f.$7 or $f.$8. In the cameras I used only the one type of film and did not experiment with any variations—the ciné cameras were only loaded with Kodachrome, the Rolleiflex with Verichrome Pan and the Leica with Kodachrome transparencies. Throughout I standardized on Kodak film and found it excellent under all conditions; it seems to me to be the most adaptable to all temperatures.

The ciné cameras had been prepared to operate in low temperatures by washing out all forms of lubrication and running the bearings 'dry'. This was only partially successful; it was satisfactory for the cameras used on Everest in 1953, but it was not good enough for temperatures below −20°F. There may be low-temperature lubricants that will not turn gluey but I feel the true answer lies in heating the camera with a small heater. Both mainsprings of the 70 D.L. cameras snapped in a temperature of −38°F when we were half-way across the continent; I completed the filming using two Bell & Howell Model 603 magazine-loaded cameras. One of these I had fitted with a heater operated from the vehicle battery circuit. I covered all the cameras with several layers of adhesive tape which helped to insulate my fingers against the cold of the metal. In temperatures below −20°F I wore three pairs of gloves—white silk gloves, soft lined leather gloves as worn by chauffeurs and elegant drivers, and heavy leather mitts slung from a neck harness with large openings into which the hands could be thrust easily.

Once silk gloves have reached the same temperature as the hands they have a remarkable insulating effect and in fact doubled the time that I could work effectively in the cold. With silk gloves I could change film and alter lens settings; with silk and leather gloves I could handle the cameras for two minutes or more before needing to thrust my hands back into the heavy working mitts which, although ungainly, were effective.

All shooting of film on the journey across the continent was a lightning skirmish. Generally without warning some action or activity would be taking place which needed recording and the cameras had to be loaded and to hand. For this I prepared camera hammocks slung inside the Weasel cab above the engine, which is beside the driver.

During the winter I filmed indoors using Type A Kodachrome. Lighting the sets was always difficult for two reasons: power from our six-kilowatt generator was rationed and the combination of five or six photofloods was too much to add to the everyday use without warning; the hut was the normal living quarters of sixteen people all busy on their own specialized work and the setting of lights could cause great inconvenience. For lighting I generally used six large photofloods about eight feet from my subject. This gave sufficient light to film with the lenses wide-open (generally $f.1\cdot8$). I had never filmed using lights of Type A before and, as with all the ciné film, I did not know if the attempts were successful until we returned to England eighteen months later.

For much of the shooting indoors I used a 10 mm. Angenieux lens. This very wide-angle lens for 16 mm. cameras was particularly useful in enclosed spaces.

For black and white pictures I used two Rolleiflex cameras. These I carried in a sponge-rubber-lined box, which stood up well to the very rough handling. Each camera had an $f.3\cdot5$

lens which I found quite adequate. One camera was a later model with the Planar lens and built-in exposure meter. For the rough expedition work I soon found the newer model was too delicate: the window of the exposure meter was soon broken and internal couplings sheared away in the cold. Allan Rogers, our doctor, who was extremely capable with small instrument work, repaired this and moulded a new window from Perspex which proved to be better than the original. I took pictures successfully with the Rolleiflex cameras in temperatures of −60°F.

I used my Leica for colour transparencies. The camera was slung round my neck on a short strap, and hung inside my outer windproof clothing. Hanging thus it was beaten and battered considerably but continued to work satisfactorily throughout the expedition. It is the 3F model, and for expedition use I prefer it to the heavier and more cumbersome M3; but it did have a disadvantage in that changing lenses in the cold was tedious.

I had two exposure meters: a Norwood and a Weston Master. In the intense cold both meters tended to become sluggish. Both were fitted with invercones which gave a truer reading than a reflected light reading from the snow. During the first year I over-exposed my shots in cloudy hazy weather in the pack ice: when the sun was obscured by low cloud the light intensity was in fact brighter than under a sunny blue sky. This was due to the cloud and snow reacting with each other to become power-ful reflectors. In the course of the journey across the continent we travelled in continuous daylight and the light values hardly changed from one week to another: I seldom referred to an exposure meter.

Before leaving England I took the opportunity of putting the cameras into a cold chamber along with a Sno-Cat. I placed in the cab of the vehicle a ciné camera, my Leica, a small Retinette, a Rolleiflex, and three box cameras, where they stayed overnight at a temperature of −45°F. Next day, when

I went in, the cameras were covered in ice and looked most unhappy. With the exception of a box camera which took successful pictures once the shutter had been pressed several times to break the internal frost, none of them worked: the intricate shutters had clogged with ice. For this reason I took six box cameras south as cold weather emergency cameras.

As it turned out a cold chamber test in England was misleading. The cameras had been taken from a warm English atmosphere and placed in the cold chamber with the moisture from the air still inside them. When the cameras were used in the Antarctic they were dry: the air was dry and the atmosphere was always below freezing-point and the cameras gave little trouble when no internal moisture was present.

At Shackleton I had a small and beautifully equipped darkroom. Kodak Limited supplied this and gave me every assistance and advice. In the basement of Kodak's in Kingsway a floor space of 6 feet by 4 feet was built with panels and into this 'mock up' were fitted an enlarger table and enlarger, a zinc-lined sink unit with splash boards, a film drying cabinet, cupboards and shelves and drying racks, with all the paraphernalia of bottles, dishes, thermometers and clocks. I worked in this darkroom for a day in London and adjustments were made. The darkroom was then dismantled and packed in such a way that all the units slipped quickly into place on arrival. Although the base hut was insulated with Fibreglass walls, the temperature gradient was generally below freezing-point at floor level, rising to over 70°F at the roof. At floor level I heated the room with a Tilley infra-red heater. For reasons of warmth I stored prepared chemicals on the shelves near the roof. With the paraffin heater burning, the temperature at waist level was about 60°F, and by raising the dishes higher I could keep them at 68°F.

Water supply in adequate quantities was a constant manual labour. Clean snow was sawn from a 'quarry' and melted down in the kitchen. I then carried this in buckets up into the attic where I installed a 25-gallon galvanized tank. This tank could be pumped to a low pressure (5 lb. per square inch) by an air pump clamped to the side. This gave a good flow of water, through a fine filter, into the darkroom. Waste water was collected in a bucket and carried outside. To conserve water I always used Kodak hypo-clearing agent.

For developing I used medium fine grain developer, Kodak D76, to process Verichrome Pan and Tri X film. For prints I used Kodak D163.

During the journey I did not process roll film but stored it in large aluminium containers and developed it in batches at South Ice, the South Pole, and Scott Base. All exposed Kodachrome was sealed in tins containing silacagel and flown to London at the end of the expedition: some of this stayed in cans for eighteen months before being processed.

PHOTOGRAPHIC EQUIPMENT

1. Ciné cameras: Two *Bell & Howell 70 D.L.*, fitted with

(a)	(i)	Bell & Howell Angenieux 10 mm. lens	($f.$ 1·8)
	(ii)	Kern 16 mm. Switar lens	($f.$ 1·8)
	(iii)	Taylor Hobson 25 mm. lens	($f.$ 1·8)
(b)	(i)	Taylor Hobson 75 mm. lens	($f.$ 2·8)
	(ii)	Kern 16 mm. Switar lens	($f.$ 1·8)
	(iii)	Kern 25 mm. Switar lens	($f.$ 1·4)

Both cameras worked well until the heavy tension springs of the clockwork motor snapped on the same day when we were half-way between the South Pole and Scott Base. These cameras had the advantage of steadiness with a long running time on the spring; but the greatest advantage came in saving weight in the film stock. Each 100-foot spool of Kodachrome weighed 7 oz., so that 10,000 feet of film stock weighed only 44 lbs.

2. Four *Bell & Howell 603 T Auto-Loads*, fitted with Taylor Hobson lenses. I had used these small magazine loading cameras on Everest and found them small and portable enough to carry easily. About two-thirds of the film *Antarctic Crossing* was taken with these small cameras. Their precision was remarkable when one considers that the 16 mm. Kodachrome was enlarged to 35 mm. and printed by Technicolor process and projected on to the 'wide' cinema screen. Into one camera was fitted a 12-volt heating unit which I adapted to plug into the vehicle batteries. Although the camera is light (weight is 4 lbs.) the film magazines are heavy. Each 50-foot magazine of Kodachrome weighed 9½ oz., so that 4,400 feet of film stock weighed 52 lbs.

3. One *Paillard Bolex H16*, fitted with

    (i) Kern 10 mm. Switar lens
    (ii) Kern 16 mm. Switar lens
    (iii) Kern 25 mm. Switar lens

This camera I used during the voyage to the Antarctic. It had not been prepared in any way for the cold conditions and ran slowly at a few degrees of frost. Because of this and its less rugged construction I sent it back in the ship. Two other Bolex H16 cameras were prepared for cold by the makers and were sent to Scott Base where Derek Wright, the photographer there, used them with marked success in temperatures down to −40°F.

4. Two *Rolleiflex*, fitted with

    (i) Zeiss Tessar 75 mm. lens $(f.3.5)$
    (ii) Planar   75 mm. lens $(f.3.5)$

5. One *Leica IIIF* fitted with

        (i) Summicron 5 cm. lens $(f.2)$
    or (ii) Summaron 3.5 cm. lens $(f.3.5)$
    or (iii) Elmar   9 cm. lens $(f.4)$

6. One *Retina II*

Amongst the other members of the party were the following cameras: five Leicas, one Contax, three Retinettes, three Retinas and one Rectaflex. Shutter trouble due to cold developed in half of these cameras.